DATE DUE

JAN 1 0 1995	
FEB 1 9 1997	
AUG 2 5 1997	
01-02-2001 *TC.* 4025950	
JUN 1 9 2015	
JUN 1 9 2015	

BUILDING PRODUCTIVE ORGANIZATIONS

THROUGH HEALTH AND WELLNESS PROGRAMS

Douglas B. Gutknecht, Ph.D.
David M. Gutknecht, M.S.

Co–Founders, The Organizational Health Promotion
and Wellness Certificate Program

UNIVERSITY PRESS OF AMERICA

Lanham • New York • London

Copyright © 1990 by

University Press of America,® Inc.

4720 Boston Way
Lanham, MD 20706

3 Henrietta Street
London WC2E 8LU England

British Cataloging in Publication Information Available

Library of Congress Cataloging-in-Publication Data

Gutknecht, Douglas B.
Building productive organizations through health
and wellness programs / by Douglas B. Gutknecht, David M. Gutknecht.
p.   cm.
Includes bibliographical references.
1. Health promotion.   2. Occupational health services.
I. Gutknecht, David M.   II. Title.
RC969.H43G88   1989   613—dc20   89–22491 CIP

ISBN 0–8191–7579–X (alk. paper)
ISBN 0–8191–7580–3 (pbk. : alk. paper)

TO CINDY, MARLEIS, MICKELLA, RENEE, ZACK AND CHRIS

TABLE OF CONTENTS

PREFACE

This book is based upon a review of large amounts of interdisciplinary literature in the fields of medical sociology, health psychology, health education, behavioral health, health prevention, public health, organizational behavior and development, human resources, stress management, marketing, and evaluation research.

It is our hope that by examining pertinent individual and organizational health promotion issues from a number of perspectives, we can develop strategies for improving the well-being and quality of life for individuals, organizations, and society. The world is changing very fast. It is imperative that we learn to apply knowledge and skills that will prepare us to proactively manage the changes in technology, community, family, work, and personal relationships and leisure so that we remain vital and healthy.

The essential image that guides the development of this text is that health prevention, promotion and enhancement must be built upon an active and productive partnership between individuals, work teams, organizations, communities and societies. This viewpoint is necessary so that we all begin to nurture a more productive and cooperative relationship between health enhancement, employee relations, traditional human resource concerns, and the larger social/public policy arena. Then decision makers at all levels of public and private life will have the substantive knowledge to risk taking the moral lead in supporting or developing programs to impact the health and quality of life crisis in the decades ahead.

Our objective is to sustain the urgency of this dialogue regarding theory, research, intervention and resource strategies that will enhance and support this interdisciplinary endeavor.

Douglas B. Gutknecht, Ph.D.
David M. Gutknecht, M.S.

Orange, California
Irvine, California
April, 1989

1

ORGANIZATIONAL HEALTH PROMOTION: IMPROVING PRODUCTIVITY AND THE QUALITY OF LIFE

INTRODUCTION

We will explore in this chapter and the next, some of the issues pertinent to taking a more organizational centered approach to health promotion (HP) and wellness. One popular definition of health promotion frequently given by the American Hospital Association seems particularly useful:

> The process of fostering awareness, influencing attitude,s and identifying
> alternatives so that individuals can make informed choices and change
> their behavior in order to achieve an optimum level of physical and men-
> tal health and improve their physical and social environment.*(Gutknecht,
> et.al., 1988)*.

We will also explore some of the assumptions that underpin a positive, bene-fits or gains-centered approach to organizational health promotion: what kind of benefits can you and your organization expect; the costs associated with ignoring personal and organizational health issues; how to develop an inte-grated and effective organizational health promotion effort; and finally, some things any organization should know before beginning a heath promotion ef-fort. It is also our responsibility as HP professionals to help educate others about the benefits and costs of sponsoring health promotion.

LIFESTYLE INFLUENCES ON U.S. MORTALITY--AN HISTORICAL PERSPECTIVE

Modern society has achieved a dramatic increase in life expectancy in the last century due to a variety of health improvements. Centuries ago people were likely to die in their 30's. The average adult in Europe in the 1500's lived to about 40 years of age. A child born in 1989 has a vastly improved chance of becoming an octogenarian. Three thousand people a day are reaching the 100 year old milestone. Between 1900 and the early 1980's the age adjusted death rate has dropped about 70% and life expectancy at birth has reached about 71.1 for males and 78.4 for females. Remember, life expectancy is usually determined at birth and again at 45 years old.

In the early part of this century the primary causes of death were infectious diseases. In descending order, these were: pneumonia and influenza; tuberculosis; small pox; and diarrhea. These contagious diseases were often spread in epidemics by poor diet, hygiene/sanitation and bacterial infections. Such events certainly affirmed the philosophy of the times that life indeed was a short and brutish affair. Between 1935 and 1954, major drug discoveries had a positive impact on the treatment of infectious diseases. Many childhood illnesses were virtually eradicated. But suddenly this dramatic decline in the mortality rate has lessened and actually worsened, particularly for certain groups.

A dramatic shift in the decline of the premature infant death rate occurred up until the early 1950's through the control of these infectious diseases and growth of public health improvements, which have much to do with our present day swing toward health promotion and wellness. This death rate began decreasing in 1900 because of public health improvements, i.e., better sanitation, improved dietary information and food practices. This decline continued until about 1954. Since that time more dramatic improvements have occurred in life expectancy of the over 45 years group. The reasons for the shift of the over 45 life expectancy has been largely attributed to a decline in cardiovascular disease through the better control of blood pressure, reductions in smoking, and consumption of high saturated fat diets, and increases in vigorous exercise. Many public health experts seem to pinpoint 1954 as the beginning of the era when life-style factors and more complex environmental factors became the primary causes of premature death and disease. We also began to hear more talk about higher mortality rates for minorities and inner city youth.

Perhaps the early 1950's was the zenith of an era of unhealthy life-style practices. About one-half of all adult Americans were smokers (of high-tar and high-nicotine cigarettes), and saturated fat consumption was high. The death rates for cancer, stroke and heart disease were still high. These events occurred at a time when physical activity, partly brought about by the phenomenon of the suburban leisure and consumption orientated family, was dominating the post Korean war lifestyle. Motor vehicle accidents also rapidly increased during this period of commuter trips to work from the growing bedroom suburbs.

In 1964, the Surgeon General's Report on the negative effects of cigarette smoking was published and became a part of the public dialogue. During the latter part of this 20-year period ending in 1974, public knowledge of the importance of preventive medicine began to take hold. We began to find more vigorous public health communications regarding the relationship between chloresterol and coronary heart disease, which positively effected the dietary habits of many Americans. In fact, this announcement in 1964 , coupled with a decline in the number of smokers (and the subsequent appearance on the market of low-tar, low-nicotine cigarettes), began having gradual effect on the mortality rate. The decrease in the American mortality rate continues to this day as an increasing percentage of Americans assume greater awareness and understanding of the many interrelated dimensions of health and well-being for themselves and others in society *(Gutknecht and Gutknecht, 1988)*.

TRADITIONAL MEDICINE AND FORCES FOR CHANGE

The traditional model of medicine is changing today. There are many internal and external reasons for these changes. Medicine is evolving partly as a result of forces from within as those long committed to preventative medicine join ranks with young doctors and dynamic leaders in the fields of preventative and behavioral medical education to propose new alternatives to the old system of both medical education and practice. In addition, external forces like changes in social, demographic, political, economic, technological and legal factors are thrusting change upon the medical establishment. Let us briefly explore some of these external reasons.

Social and Demographic factors are the consequences of shifts in the population, such as the increases in those of the baby-boom generation or cohort (born between 1946-1964) or those in old age (over 65), that have social implications for other institutions, such as health, education and work.

Demographics also influence how each of us experiences well-being and wellness because of the relationship of population to our ability to accomplish personally meaningful goals.

In order to understand what we mean, picture society as a large python that swallows a large pig (a large population group like the baby-boomers or the aged). This pig is a food bulge (like a population bulge) that then moves through the entire length of the python's body. The consequences of such large numbers of individuals reaching certain ages at the same time has an enormous impact upon health, financial, and retirement policies of our society. We can observe that the large number of individuals in a birth cohort (born about the same time) often contribute to competition for jobs and pay raises, which can then lead to work-related stress and a number of other social problems.

Consider another example of a demographic trend is our aging population. As the growth of medical institutions has contributed to the "graying" of America by reducing death rates from acute or infectious disease, medical practice has also shifted the attention of society from a worry about reduced life-expectancy to a concern with prolonging life through expensive medical technology. This may occur at the expense of considering quality-of-life issues. But a question remains regarding the ability of society to pay the costs of taking care of this group in the long-term, using an antiquated, disease-based model of medicine.

Demographic changes have also impacted residential and racial patterns and helped reduced the importance of extended family support networks. This social fact has greatly increased the problems of treating the poor and actually caused certain hospitals mandated to treat the poor to assume ever larger deficits. This trend has led to the emergence of counter trends, such as self-care through medical books, personal health monitoring, the turning of the human potential movement toward preventive health and the rapid growth of health education, health promotion and wellness lifestyle consulting.

Political and economic issues of health practice have grown in importance recently. The health of any nation is strongly linked with its economy and resource base, the politics of professional associations, and the political influence of corporations which market medical products and drugs.

A proliferation of new medical techniques and technologies that were invented to reduce costs, now cause an inflationary surge in health care costs, at the same time that general inflationhas been relatively low. In addition other trends are emerging to limit inflationary cost increases such as alternative birth centers, which can cut the time and costs of post-birth hospitalization by limiting drug use and encouraging more active involvement on the part of both parents, shortening the stay. *Paul Starr (1982)* argues that the cost concerns impacting society, corporations and even hospitals themselves will, in the long-run, limit the practice of traditional disease-based medicine.

Finally, the importance of legal influences on health institutions--traditional and non-traditional--should not be discounted. For example, licensing laws for new categories of health professionals, like physicians' and nurses' assistants, can have profound impacts upon the ability of the medical world to continue business as usual. In addition, the creation of such legislative entities as Health System Agencies (HSA) can examine the possibilities of sharing the expensive technology among local hospitals.

THE EMERGENCE OF THE HOLISTIC HEALTH MOVEMENT

The first period of fairly substantial growth of what we now regard as the wellness or organizational health promotion movement began with the human potential and holistic health movements of the 1960's. We have difficulty writing of the contemporary wellness movement and workplace health promotion without a brief look at some of their ideas.

Before the term "health promotion" was conceived, a number of health professionals and enlightened physicians began to reject the limitations of the traditional medical model. They realized that by the time many individuals were symptomatic for a particular diagnosis, the disease had already taken root and progressed enough to impact the person's quality of existence. In many situations the disease did not even have a physical/biological origin. In addition, for some physicians their treatment options seemed limited because the problems seemed more related to lifestyle related conditions.

Many physicians and health professionals were reminded that the cure was often worse than the disease. That is, the side effects of treatment (iatrogenesis) for many diseases produced secondary symptoms as painful and as problematic as the original disease. Also, various social movements, such as women's health groups, consumer groups, advocates of naturalness in diet/exercise, human potential practitioners, the handicapped, the poor and other minorities left out of the traditional system by discrimination or lack of access, all contributed to this discussion. Some segments of this group were ostracized by certain sectors of the medical community for supporting and/or practicing the "art" and not the "science" of healing/medicine. However, one key principle has gained substantial acceptance and that is the philosophy of prevention. Some believe today that the valuable holistic health ideas have already been "digested" by mainstream medicine, with the useful parts being assimilated and the more controversial aspects being discarded. Still, some dubious holistic practitioners, promising more than than they can deliver and appealing to (and preying on) the emotion and superstition of a segment of the vulnerable ailing, are practicing "quackery" under the guise of "anything goes " holistic medicine. We must examine some of the trends in this area.

DEFINITION OF HOLISTIC HEALTH
Weil (1983) defines holistic health "as an informal collection of attitudes and practices, not a defined system of treatment." *Pelletier (1979)* defines it as a "medical orientation that acknowledges that each state of health and disease requires a consideration of all contributing factors: psychological, psychosocial, environmental, and spiritual." *Weil (1983:181)* does not like the terms, "holistic health," preferring "homeopathy or natural medicine," because "the word [holistic] has become a loaded term that pushes the emotional buttons of many people, particularly conservative practioners of traditional medicine, in much the same way as 'natural' does."

Competent holistic health practitioners subscribe to the principle that regardless of the condition (or prevention classification) of an individual's health, he/she can, and should, be treated from a holistic perspective. *Weil (1983)* has listed the five most common dimensions these practioners utilize:
1. The mind, body and spirit are all involved in positive health.
2. Responsibility for health lies with the individual.
3. The M.D. should act as consultant, not a commander.
4. Health is more than the absence of disease.
5. Natural healing is a preferable health strategy to surgery and drugs.

CRITICISMS OF HOLISTIC PRACTITIONERS
One can infer from some of the above discussions that holistic practitioners

are more prone to mismanage medical problems. I doubt that this true for most of those trained and practicing what they call holistic medicine. Much holistic treatment is not an alternative to medical care but a revision of the disease-based model of medicine that is in line with what many call preventive medicine. Another criticism of the holistic model is that there is inadequate scientific evidence to support effectiveness. Research is limited at this point because of the newness of the treatment modality. However, substantial clinical research relating to certain behavioral aspects of preventive care are constantly being evaluated, and growing support is validating the general model. *Weil (1983:182)* is more accurate in his criticisms. First, is the assertion that the general movement has no theoretical unity or coherence, lending itself to misuse and overblown claims for the many possibly valuable but limited practices. Second, is the claim that doctors who label themselves holistic are uncritically accepting of some of the more unorthodox practices of holistic medicine. Weil mentions the technique of "applied kinesiology" in the latter category, which "uses muscle resistance as an indicator of organ weakness and intolerance to foods and drugs."

OBSTACLES TO ACCEPTANCE OF A PREVENTIVE APPROACH

If we as a society are in the midst of a change in the traditional way we receive medical care and delivery, why does it seem that we are moving at a snail's pace? With more interest on the part of management and an increasing number of the general public embracing many of these new ideas regarding behavioral health and lifestyle choices, still seem unable to make necessary lifestyle changes. *Pelletier (1985)* explains why this is so:

1. Traditionally held beliefs resist change. Our present system reflects our society's values, beliefs, and symbols. Consumers of medical care bear substantial responsibility for creating the very medical care system which they condemn.

2. Medical consumers have unrealistic expectations. They have demanded a medical system based upon expectations of medical intervention and then have become indignant and hostile when these expectations are left unfulfilled.

3. The public is slow to recognize why health care costs have risen. While virtually all medical consumers are appalled by the rapid escalating costs of medical care, few clearly see the connection between this rise and the fact that the greatest portion of the national expenditure for medical care is for premature, i.e., preventable, disorders.

4. Substance abuse problems, among other symptoms of excessive lifestyle indulgences, are rampant in our affluent society. Also, expensive health care is itself a sign of affluence for

those who can afford it or have access to insurance in lieu of other symbols of wealth, and have the attitude that "we're not really paying for it anyway." A major impediment to improved national health is such often ignorant and even self-destructive behavior patterns pervasive in our culture.

5.   Leadership from our medical community has been slow in coming. Less than 2.5% of our total medical expenditures go for prevention and about .5% is spent on health education.

6.   Increased technology has produced more medical specialists. Excessive specialization of physicians works against the basic idea of preventive health.

7.   Medical consumers have not been held accountable for their spending. Another barrier to change is the payment policies of medical insurance. Approximately 90% of our population is covered by medical insurance and therefore most medical care is paid for by "third parties." These systems are pathology oriented with virtually no incentives for prevention.

Accordingly, wellness and health promotion are not concepts with meaning just for individuals and organizations. The relevance of health promotion is in its application to group, family, community and society. In fact, it is much easier to ensure personal health when we are supported by well-functioning, optimally healthy systems at other social levels. We also need to clearly understand the impact these other systems have upon our health and adaptive capabilities.

The U.S. Center for Disease Control estimates that about 50% of all deaths under 65 years old are related to lifestyle excesses. This finding is supported by the *1975 Framingham Study* which identified the proportional impact of the four leading contributors to early death and diseases. The four primary contributors are *(Gutknecht, et.al.,1988)*:

1. Lifestyle   53%
2. Environment 21%
3. Heredity   16%
4. Medical care 10%

Researchers now believe that preventive, active, and integrated approaches to health promotion can have a positive influence on at least the first and last categories. Other research on accidents, suicides and homicides generally confirms the estimation of mortality for factors of social and life-style influences.

We should not not take anything for granted, but it seems fairly obvious that the place where we work, spend so much of out time and derive so much of our self-esteem, should become the primary focus of our attack. I guess a more appropriate question might be: Why hasn't this approach taken hold sooner and without the obvious starts and stops that we have historically observed?

HEALTH, AND WELLNESS?

The most common, traditional definition of "health" is the dictionary definition: "free from sickness." Many still harbor the inaccurate belief that if we are not sick, then we must be healthy. Personal health care is defined through formal visits to the doctor when we are sick. This ritual legitimates our absence from work; we enter, in the language of sociologists the "sick role" with all the accompanying rights and often ignored obligations. Virtually all health benefits are designed to reward sickness and disease, not productive health and living. Our health care system might be more accurately labeled a "disease care" system. In contrast, promoting health as wellness simply means taking an active interest in our total life and effectiveness while we are healthy. This process requires us to identify and change lifestyle habits that place us at risk for contracting certain degenerative diseases as we age. Thus, the quality of life decreases as we age, rather than becoming a time for full enjoyment of our multiple opportunities. In this definition, health and wellness always include a zest for living life to its fullest. This concept is not new; it was very effectively reintroduced by Halbert Dunn, among others, in the 1950's. Dunn's concept of optimum wellness was based upon the World Health Organization's definition of health *(Dunn, 1961)*. Dunn maintained that traditional health failed to give us much of a protective edge because it was only a passive state of homeostasis or equilibrium, while the process of wellness was a more dynamic condition of movement toward a higher health potential. Dunn's argument is not very controversial today but in the fifties it sounded very progressive. The definition of wellness relating to three areas:

1. The direction of progress;
2. The involvement of the total individual;
3. The way that the individual adapts.

This first idea is that movement is toward a goal of higher or optimal functioning, implying that wellness is an active and self-directed process of choosing to improve one's quality of existence. The second concept develops an image of the well-functioning, healthy and integrated person who has met their needs in several areas of existence. The third idea is that the highly functioning person is able to anticipate and handle a world of change.

The above three concepts can serve as our starting point for a journey to higher levels of health. Of course, we must recognize that this view is a major reversal of the traditional model of health. Recently however, more innovative health professionals, and educators, health promotion consultants, cost-conscious CEO's of major companies, and progressive, small business people have become more interested in any available techniques for improving the quality of life, productivity and profitability of their organizations. Companies now see the need to explore how promoting personal awareness and responsibility for individual health can contribute to a longer-term solution to healthier bottom line. The trend toward more personal accountability has created a climate for positive change in organizations.

One recent survey shows the extent to which people are currently becoming involved in their own health care. The changes toward self-management have been significant. The following are a few of the highlights from this survey:

- Between 1970 and 1986, consumption of whole milk fell by 60%, while the consumption of lowfat milk products increased by 83%.

- Between 1970 and 1986, sales of yogurt a decaffeinated coffee increased by over 250%.
- From 1977 to 1986, sales of self-care books increased by more than 1,500%.

- Over 30% of adults say they are committed to a prevention lifestyle to some degree to.

- Over 40% of visits to doctors are to obtain advice and information which is readily available in self-help books and magazines.

The authors estimate that $25 billion of services now provided by health professionals could probably be replaced by self-care and preventive measures. *(Gutknecht and Gutknecht, 1988)*

THE WELLNESS CONTINUUM
This continuum represents a summation of several authors' attempts to simplify the whole concept of wellness. In theory, we are all at some point on this continuum at all times.

WELLNESS CONTINUUM MODEL

TRADITIONAL MEDICINE   **HEALTH
                                                                            PROMOTION**

[SYMPTOMS RISKS] [EDUCATION   BEHAVIOR CHANGE]
PREMATURE   **TOTAL
DEATH**   [DISABILITY]   [MOTIVATION]   **WELL
                                                                            BEING**

>>>>>>>>>>>>>>>>>>>+++++++++++++++++X+++++++++++++++>>>>>>>>>>>>>>>>>
                              MIDPOINT

It is important to remember that where you areright now is not necessarily where you will be next year. Traditional medical practice, represented by the left side of the continuum, supports the treatment of health problems, often of a serious or chronic nature, after they have occurred (reactive). The middle point of this continuum represents the absence of major diseases. Most of us are probably at or near this mid-point. We view ourselves as being healthy since we have no visible signs or symptoms of disease. People who fall on the right side of the diagram are those who constantly seek to educate themselves, motivate and apply new knowledge to increase their overall health and personal productivity. If 100 average Americans were asked where they fell on this continuum, many would likely overstate their current health condition.

Since our definition of active health and wellness indicates a long-term process of learning to take personal control of one's health and well-being, slow but steady progress should not be confused with promised results of short-term fads or even with your current state of health. You may also be in excellent health without actively knowing that you are practicing a wellness lifestyle. Conversely, you may become vigorous in your pursuit of a healthy life, yet still have some health problems as a result of your heredity, poor health behaviors in early life, or lack of knowledge concerning strategies for reducing health risk factors and maintaining positive behavioral changes. For this reason, awareness through education and health assessment is only the first important step.

The goal of effective health promotion programs is to maximize flexibility, choice and personal responsibility throughout the organization. This process requires a comprehensive approach to optimal functioning, including health choices and work performance. When employees feel the negative health effects of inconsistent and unclear work policies, poorly-designed jobs and rapidly increasing stress levels, disability claims increase dramatically. In such situations, organizations should not assume that simply providing adequate insurance benefits, or adding copayments, will solve the problems of excessive health care utilization, increased health care costs, absenteeism, and turnover.

These problems are often inherent in the design of the organizational culture, policies and structures. Such problems must be addressed as leadership, management and human resources or training issues that are intimately related to other issues such as low productivity and poor work quality. This total organizational approach demands a long-range approach. Let us become proactive and not wait for a crisis that requires us to react with half-hearted and half-planned efforts and programs.

ENLARGING PERSONAL CHOICE AND RESPONSIBILITY

Improving one's health is related to the opportunity to maximize one's potential and enlarge one's possibilities for self-knowledge, emotional balance, physical fitness, intellectual/mental effectiveness and work productivity. True health or wellness is more than just reacting to daily choices by avoiding life style risks. Living brings everyone numerous stresses and pressures. We each have the option of actively anticipating and responding to these events as opportunities for change and improvement, or merely waiting and reacting to events as they occur. The former choice is based upon the idea that a pro-active health and wellness path is available to each us, and by following it we can learn to improve the quality of our life as we age. Although we must accept biological limits to our health and our lifespan, the key is to improve the quality of existence over an increasing span of years until death. Aging and mortality demand that we think about the future quality of existence for ourselves and our children. The consequence of blocking the possibilities for improving our health and quality of life as we age is loss of that sense of purpose and meaningful involvement that should sustain us through our latter years. By blocking opportunities for responsible involvement and choice, we elevate a narrow definition of what health and life can become as we age.

If we accept the idea of the inevitable decline in our health then we will retreat into reactive and defensive thinking as individuals. Organizations will likewise fail to grasp the tremendous potential for both short- and long- range impacts upon their organizations. Anxious, neurotic and preoccupied, people and organizations will try to escape the costs of avoiding these important questions. We can try to rationalize and make short-term economic and political excuses for the costs of failing to set important priorities for our nation's health and quality of life. This strategy has allowed organizations to avoid any responsibility and is no longer a viable option. We know that the problems are too interdependent to place blame at either the individual or organizational levels. We also know that someone always pays the piper for these costs associated with our affluent-orientated lifestyles and disease-oriented health care system.

We have a public duty to think about the consequences of our choices, whether personal or social. Organizations have an excellent opportunity to provide the leadership to share information and resources that will help the average worker to aspire to improved health and wellness, leading to more effective performance and productivity in many other spheres of their personal and work lives. Organizational health promotion and wellness are more than mere physical health; they are quality-of-life issues and, thus, impact our total well-being.

THE WORKPLACE HEALTH PROMOTION IMPERATIVE

The positive impact of increasing personal accountability and involvement on the overall American workforce has a long way to go before we can let up the pressure. In fact, the momentum for a revolution in wellness is now substantial. Some of the negative statistics have motivated companies of all sizes to show an increasing interest in workplace health promotion and employee development:

> Twenty-nine million workdays are lost annually due to hypertension, stroke, and coronary heart disease; thirty percent of the 100 million U.S. workers suffer from high blood pressure and are risk for developing strokes, heart and/or kidney disease; over 30% of the U.S. population still smokes, and smokers have a much higher risk for many diseases; about 10% of the workforce can be classified as problem employees *(Gutknecht and Gutknecht, 1988)*.

Health care now consumes more than one out of every nine dollars earned by the average worker, meaning that they must work over one month each year to pay these costs. Employers now pay half of the nation's health bill which accounts for 10% of the total compensation to employees. General Motors revealed that over $400 of the cost of a 1984 GM car was the result of health care costs for employees. Companies are spending over $700 million annually to replace the more than 200,000 men between the ages of 45 and 65 who are killed or disabled by coronary heart disease.

Most chief executive officers (CEOs) are concerned about upward national trends in health care costs, particularly those that impact their own company. Reports, similar to the following one from the Harvard Business Review, are difficult to ignore and are very disturbing to progressive companies.

> Company expenses for health care are rising at such a fast rate that if unchecked, within eight years will eliminate all profits for the average "Fortune 500" company and the largest 250 industrials. From 1981 to 1983, the average rate of increase of health insurance premiums for these companies was a staggering 20%, and health care costs amounted to 24% of average corporate profits after taxes. Although the rates of cost increase moderated in 1984, their growth was still much higher than that of the Consumer Price Index *(Herzlinger and Calkins, 1986)*.

INVESTING IN PEOPLE

Organizational health promotion will help any organization to manage itself more productively. Using the language of profits and investment, we are investing in the maintenance of our human capital for enhancing productivity. Just as we invest in the maintenance of physical capital for profits, we invest in our workers' good health. A profitable company is never defined as one that is not losing money, so good health should not be defined as not being sick . However, when business strategies are being developed, the inclusion of people as an important organizational asse, is only given lip service. *Yavitch (1988: 35-40)* suggests that there are three reasons for ignoring people as the primary assets:

First, in historical perspective, Taylor and other proponents of Scientific Management emphasized human labor as a cost component, ignoring their role as an important determinant of production strategy.

Second, a more pervasive factor is the treatment of human assets in conventional accounting practices. Employees are designated in the operating statement as a variable (short-term, readily liquidated and easily reacquired) expense. These conventions are followed by the same organizations who have supported a short-term outlook. In an uncertain international marketplace, however, we need to rethink these conventions along the lines of those productive companies who view employees as a long-term asset, whose proper maintenance is an obligation of doing business.

The third reason is the basic difficulty of analyzing, measuring and quantifying the components that comprise human resources:

1. What is the "productive capacity" of a worker?

2. At what point is the limit of a worker's talent or capability reached? Is this a limit on the volume of work he or she can handle?

Some researchers, such as *Odiorne (1986)* have tried to surmount these difficulties by developing a portfolio approach to categorizing human assets. In this view, people are categorized as productive stars, workhorses, problem employees, and cash cows. Although this view sounds callous, at least it can force organizations to begin to think of ways to maintain and help develop their human assets, so they can perform productively and return their investment over the longest period possible. This strategy should start us thinking about how we can utilize new development strategies to show that healthy and effectively trained people do make a difference to our eventual success.

We must also make a distinction between machines and people. Machines periodically break even with the best maintenance, while people are capable of keeping healthy over their lives with the proper maintenance. People can rebound from failure and retrain themselves for future successful performance. Although people are renewable, they are not infinitely so. Once neglect and extensive damage start the process of long-term degeneration, the process of healing produces more marginal results for people. The failure to care for our assets, whether physical or human, produces both direct and indirect costs to the organization. This fact is often ignored when discussing human resources because an unhealthy workplace produces costs that are often submerged in a narrow view of fixed assets. It is easier to think of investing in machinery maintenance than people maintenance.

THE COSTS OF IGNORING INVESTMENT IN PEOPLE

Let us document some of costs that result from ignoring this investment in people: costs related to salary, medical treatment, rehabilitation, survivor benefits, workers compensation, distress, pay for temporary workers, overtime for others, training, retraining, rehabilitation for workers who resume work after long absences, turnover, recruitment, selection, hiring replacements and administrative overhead. We know that by investing in human resource and health promotion activities, organizations can better control their risk factors associated with disease and productivity sapping costs.

The following factors reduce personal life expectancy, worker morale, organizational productivity, and the quality of life for all workers: eating, smoking or drinking excessively; failing to adequately communicate or to resolve work conflicts; designing jobs poorly or giving poor performance. We cannot continue to ignore the consequences of our limited investments in people's health and well-being without creating such unwanted products as troubled employees and lowered productivity. Two conservative estimates of the overall financial impact of troubled employees on the average company are that:

1. 18% of any workforce causes 25% loss of productivity.
2. 10% of any workforce is causes 37.5% loss of productivity.

These productivity percentage estimates are based on such measurable factors as absenteeism, sick leave, accidents, and rising health benefits claims. The estimates do not include the hidden costs of poor decisions, corporate theft, decrease in quality of work produced, early retirement, and workers' compensation claims. Five other cost categories to business are listed below *(Gutknecht and Gutknecht,1988)*:

1. **The Economic Costs**
   A. Alcoholism is costing U.S. industry more than $20.6 billion a year in lost productivity.
   B. The cost of lost productivity due to drug abuse is nearly $16.6 billion a year.
   C. Illness, both mental and physical, resulting from occupational stress costs U.S. business an estimated $20 billion a year in the white collar job sector alone.
   D. The total costs to industry, based on the conservative dollar estimates of lost productivity listed above, surpass $55 billion for alcohol, drug, and mental health.

2. **The Personnel Costs**
   A. Sick leave taken.
   B. Absenteeism.
   C. On-the-job accidents.
   D. Leave without pay.
   E. Absence without leave.
   F. Suspension related to emotional or addiction problems.
   G. Replacement costs.
   H. Termination costs.

3. **The Health Care Costs**
   A. Health insurance claims.
   B. Sick benefit payments.
   C. Accident benefits paid.

    D. Outpatient medical visits.
    E. Inpatients medical days.
    F. Disability retirement and early retirement related to personal reasons.
    G. Workers' compensation claims related to personal reasons.

4. The Hidden Costs
    A. Bad business decisions.
    B. Diverted supervisory and managerial time.
    C. Friction among workers.
    D. Damage to equipment.
    E. Personnel turnover.
    F. Damage to public image.

5. Additional Costs to Industry
    A. Discipline and grievance action (legal).
    B. Productivity losses (decline in performance functioning).
    C. Corporate theft.
    D. Threat to public safety.

THE BENEFITS OF INVESTING IN PEOPLE

The organizational benefits are: creating a more satisfied and productive workforce; reducing health care costs, disability and worker's compensation claims that are associated with life-style related behavior; and reductions in employee turnover, absenteeism, poor morale, negative worker attitudes, and dysfunctional group norms. In the final analysis the cultural norms of the work environment and the standards of acceptable managerial behavior will support or detract from a more healthy, effective, and productive orientation. This organizational support will then help sustain positive lifestyle changes.

By building a strong health promotion effort, human resource, and an employee assistance people can begin to work together to reduce the many costs associated with poor productivity, health/life-style excesses, and employee problems. The savings from reducing poor health, ineffective performance, lost productivity and personal distress can never be measured precisely. But we can measure and evaluate some of the savings that will have a positive effect on work group and overall productivity (more on this topic in chapters 2, 3 & 9).

The personal benefits are both immediate and long-term because, as one gradually feels healthier today, the cumulative effect is the avoidance of long-term degenerative diseases. There is also improved knowledge, attitudes and behaviors about other areas of life, in addition to increased knowledge about poor health habits and their associated risks. Improved life satisfaction results from this increased knowledge of more effective behavior. This occurs when the individual starts to support the need to take personal responsibility for the conditions that lead to poor health and low vitality. Being sick in the traditional medical sense (pathology model) provides a limited vantage point for promoting a long-term view for positive health. This occurs because when we are ill we enter the "sick role." We have learned early that as long as we go to the doctor and then follow the prescribed regimen for treating symptoms, we can remain home from work, free of guilt. We feel little personal accountability for understanding how or why we became ill in the first place. This is not only costly to the organization, but may also perpetuate continued illness behavior (including absenteeism and worker compensation claims for stress).

ORGANIZATIONAL HEALTH PROMOTION ISSUES

Organizational health promotion is the term most often used when discussing the application of health and wellness strategies and principles (including the behavioral changes discussed in chapter 3 and elsewhere) to institutions and organizations. Health promotion can be defined as the systematic efforts by institutions and organizations to prevent illness, disease or premature death of its employees through education, behavior change, and cultural and organizational supports. Organizational health promotion is a strategic effort to reduce the health and lifestyle risks of employees through planned changes in individual behaviors and other predisposing conditions in the organization. The concern is with facilitating the process of good interaction and communication, as well as building more effective and productive organizations. Let us reduce this definition to more manageable ideas.

A health promotion program is a process set up in your organization to help your employees to achieve a healthier, more effective lifestyle. Each employee must be made aware that their everyday habits and choices (whether eating, sleeping, working, smoking, exercise) and their current physical condition (blood pressure, HDL and cholesterol levels) will put them at risk for certain diseases. This means that lifestyle choices and action habits may increase the chances of our dying early or experiencing a lessened quality of life as we age. The three most prominent risk factors are hypertension, high cholestero and smoking. Other prominent risk factors are diabetes, obesity, physical inactivity, poor diet, excessive alcohol consumption and, high stress.

Remember that health promotion is more than risk reduction; it is a means of optimally improving the quality of your life. If we use this definition, we may also guardedly use the wellness concept. The key principle is that people, as well as all work systems, are capable of making significant improvements by using proper assessment, planning, thoughtful implementation strategies, feedback, marketing and evaluation. Wellness and health promotion efforts, therefore, are not final achievements that once reached are then self-perpetuating, but are rather part of an ongoing process that requires a resourceful, disciplined, sustained and organizationally relevant commitment. Thus, health promotion must focus upon new approaches that not only stimulate, motivate and inspire workers, but also help organizations and workers to recognize their mutual interests and the productive potential of working together (see chapter 2).

THREE LEVELS OF ORGANIZATION HEALTH PROMOTION

There are three levels of organizational health promotion programs that correspond to the stages of individual health promotion which will be discussed in chapter 3. Let us briefly review these stages.

The **first level** is focused upon awareness and information contained in introductory talks about health promotion or payroll stuffers on changing negative health behaviors.

The **second level** is general health information, along with structured programs, i.e., hypertension control screenings and Health Risk Appraisals (HRA). These programs serve to determine risk factors or predisposition to disease. This program level tries to help the individual to consolidate some of the information gained through awareness at the first level.

The **third level** of programs is composed of fairly comprehensive health promotion activities that utilize intervention systems for promoting ongoing behavioral change. These interventions for maintaing personal improvements begun in the last stage through human resource incentives, rewards and supporting policies. The third level is also concerned with promoting organizational change, work redesign, cultural change, and changes of organizational philosophy, values, norms, and management styles.

We must learn how to make our organizational cultures promote and support positive values, health promotion and life-long personal, organizational and community wellness. We must become more aware of the destructive trends that impact society, organizations and individual lives. We can accomplish these productivity enhancing goals only by viewing the organization as an interdependent, open system that has structural, policy and behavioral health components.

COMPONENTS OF HEALTH PROMOTION

Health promotion planners often develop too narrow a focus for organizational wellness system activities. To fully understand a comprehensive perspective, we have listed below the main categories and programs that any health promotion system should provide. Please feel free to expand upon any of the following topics and continue to supplement them throughout the course *(Gutknecht and Gutknecht,1988)*:

1. **Self-Care Practices**
   A. Breast Self-Exam.
   B. Blood PressureSself-Monitoring.
   C. Healthy Back Care.

2. **Reduced Use of Harmful Substances**
   A. Alcohol Education.
   B. Drug Abuse Awareness.
   C. Smoking Cessation.

3. **Individual Safety Practices**
   A. Workplace Safety Practices.
   B. First Aid and CPR.
   C. Safe Driving Practices.

4. **Coping Skills**
   A. Stress Management.
   B. Time Management.
   C. Positive Self-Image.

5. **Fitness**
   A. Aerobic Exercise.
   B. Fitness Testing.
   C. Weight Reduction.

6. **Nutrition**
   A. Diet Analysis.

    B. Nutrition Education and Modification.

7. **Appropriate Use of the Health System Benefits**
   A. Health Insurance Utilization Education.
   B. Benefits Review.

8. **Patient Compliance**
   A. Diabetes Control.
   B. Hypertension Control.
   C. Heart Disease Education.

9. **Consumer Education**
   A. Food Label Reading.
   B. Seat Belt Safety.
   C. Athletic Equipment Education (i.e., shoes).

10. **Medical Screenings**
    A. Health Risk Appraisals.
    B. Multiphasic Screenings.
    C. Cholesterol Testing.

11. **Workplace Policies**
    A. Smoke-free Workplace.
    B. Personnel Policies (i.e., sick leave).
    C. Healthy Foods Program.
    D. Reward Policies

ORGANIZATIONAL HEALTH PROMOTION TODAY

Today, over 50,000 companies offer various health and fitness programs. About half of American companies with 50 or more employees have some sort of wellness program. Most of these have their origin during the 1970's as a result of attempts to deal with executive and managerial stress, heart disease, burnout and other health factors related to costly early retirements, turnover, recruitment and training, as well as premature and untimely deaths of key personnel. As these programs grew and were extended, it became clear that they could produce gains in productivity, reduce health care claims, and increase worker satisfaction. A survey of wellness programs by *Solomon (Gutknecht,et.al.,1988)* revealed some interesting results:

1. The most common type of company with a wellness program was in the consumer goods sector, while the least common was in the manufacturing sector.

2. Eighty-nine percent of the 28 companies who responded to the survey had fairly diverse goals, including:

	Company Goals	No.
A.	Reducing health care costs	16
B	Increasing productivity	13
C.	Improving performance	11
D	Enhancing the company's image	9
E.	Protecting the employee	9
F.	Boosting morale	8
G.	Aiding recruitment	5

A Gallup Poll several years ago indicated that 62% of employees who began exercising stated that they found new energy, while 46% said they felt more confident, 44% experienced greater job satisfaction, and 37% reported increased levels of creativity in the office. Further, an experiment conducted with NASA employees found that 50% of their employees who adhered faithfully to an exercise program reported more positive attitudes toward their jobs *(Gutknecht, et.al.,1988)*.

CAN HEALTH PROMOTION AT WORK REALLY WORK?

As an environment for promoting health lifestyle changes, the workplace represents advantages not found in other settings. Some of the advantages detailed by one research team are included in the following:

1. The employees represent a captive audience. They can be contacted and recruited at little cost to the employer.

2. Workplace populations include individuals normally unlikely to seek professional help for personal problems.

3. Work settings are most often more convenient for participants than community-based facilities.

4. The social and organizational characteristics of the workplace may increase treatment effectiveness.

5. Workplace programs, done well, can reduce health care costs. This can benefit both employer and employee.

6. Health promotion programs are inexpensive, yet often viewed as an employee benefit *(Gutknecht and Gutknecht,!988)*.

ASSESSING HP NEEDS AND INTERESTS

The primary purpose of this first step is to gather data describing employee health, health care costs, absenteeism, and turnover. These utilization and other expenditure patterns are examined along with employee attitudes toward their work and proposed health promotion activities. Management involvement is essential during this early developmental phase.

ESTABLISHING GOALS FOR HP EFFORTS

Clearly written goals are essential for effective implementation and long-term evaluation of company health promotion efforts. These goals can be expressed in numerous ways. One goal might be to decrease the utilization of health care resources by X% over the next several years. Another might be to involve a certain percentage of the workforce in one or more activities during a given year. If the company wants to implement a smoke-free workplace, the goal might be to reduce the number of total smokers through smoking cessation activities prior to the new policy taking effect. Goals of the program must reflect some of the reasons why the company originally began a health promotion program. Five of the most often cited reasons are:

1. To help contain health care costs,
2. To increase productivity and morale,
3. To better manage human resources,
4. To comply with health and safety regulations, and
5. To foster a better public and organizational image.

PLANNING THE HP EFFORT

Preparatory activities will center on a variety of critical details and questions: How much money, time, and human resources will be allotted to health promotion? What programs will be conducted? When and where will they be held? Who will deliver them? How will employees be attracted to these activities? How can quality be assured? What evaluation criteria will be used to measure effectiveness? How can community resources be utilized?

IMPLEMENTATION OF HP ACTIVITIES

If the groundwork has been properly layed, the program director will be able to concentrate on logistical details and intercompany marketing efforts to maximize program involvement. The range of interventions coming under a broad definition of health promotion or wellness include: employee assistance programs, health promotion newsletters, back injury prevention, first aid, CPR, weight reduction, nutrition, smoking cessation, implementation of a smoke-free workplace, safety programs, cancer screenings, high blood pressure programs, stress management, physical fitness, health risk appraisals, and many more that meet the criteria specified.

EVALUATING YOUR HP PROGRAM

Evaluation actually begins during the planning phase because decisions made at that time will determine how later measurements of success or failure are applied.

Voluntary Health Risk Appraisals (HRA) are commonly given to all interested employees at the beginning of a program. At the end of the first year, another HRA is given and the two are compared. The results answer the question, "Have participants significantly reduced one or more risk factors as a result of health promotion activities?" Is there a difference between those who participated in health promotion activities and those who only took the HRAs? Is the HRA itself an intervention? Do participants' risk factor reduction scores correlate with reduced utilization of health care resources? This last question may take several years to answer.

Pen and Pencil Questionnaires are also frequently used, often concurrently with HRAs, to evaluate attitudes and behaviors of participating and non-participating employees. Questions may include, "How did you like this activity?" "How much has this intervention effected your behavior?" "Was it long enough?" "How effective were the communications announcing the program?" The two questions that each program director must ask to evaluate health promotion efforts are, "Is this Program effective?" and "What is (or will be) its cost-benefit?" The question of effectiveness will involve a broad evaluation of program factors, including improved, long-term organizational functioning, increased morale, reduced absenteeism, and turnover. These factors do influence the bottom line, but cost influences are seen over a longer time frame. The keys to successful cost effectiveness are diligence, patience, monitoring and feedback.

CONTRIBUTING CAUSES OF HEALTH CARE COST INCREASES

Health care costs have outgained the annual inflation rate for at least the last five years. In 1950, health care amounted to 4.4% of the GNP, by 1984 this figure had risen to almost 11% or $388 billion. If this trend continues at 10% annually (a figure well below the recent rate of increase), the U.S. will be spending $1.7 trillion per year on health care at the end of the century, or almost $5,500 per person *(Herlinger and Calkins,1986).*

The following are among the factors contributing to the upward trend in health care costs and have led us to where we are today.

1.   An increasing proportion of the American workforce now has medical coverage.

2.   Benefit and reimbursement levels have increased for most employees in the last decade due to collective bargaining and the need to attract and retain good employees.

3.   The traditional third party payer process (i.e., insurance carriers) does not hold the consumers of health care resources directly accountable, resulting in over-utilization.

4.   A portion of the cost for Medicare and Medicaid patients has been shifted to the private sector. In hospitals, prospective payment (a predetermined amount based on the diagnosis) for Medicare patients has generally led to more costly hospital stays for regular insurance patients (often called "cost-shifting").

5.   Medical malpractice litigation against physicians and medical institutions has tended to produce a defensive style of medical practice often characterized by over-utilization of laboratory and other services to prevent lawsuits.

6.   Technology-intensive health services keep people alive longer at a higher cost, and with technology, equipment, and facilities that quickly become obsolete.

HEALTH PROMOTION AS COST-CONTAINMENT

Health promotion as a health care cost containment tool can best be viewed as a company investment paying long-term dividends. One researcher states that "organizations seeking only short-term solutions to the health care cost crisis, and failing to invest some of those savings in long-range programs such as health promotion, will find themselves on a gradient of escalating health care costs equal to that preceding the cost containment effort" *(Herrlinger and Calkins,1986).* The cost containment curve will abate only when a company reinvests wisely in health promotion.

The research evidence is now accumulating to support the belief that workplace health promotion can produce economic savings for employers. Two recent literature reviews, have found evidence that a number of programs can save employers money by reducing health care, disability, or absenteeism costs. Some of these type programs include the following: stress management, alcohol and drug abuse control, hypertension control, colorectal and breast cancer screening, smoking cessation, physical fitness, weight management, nutrition, and back injury prevention. However, other researchers are quick to point out that most of the data relating to cost are descriptive in nature and are not derived from long-term, controlled studies. This is a common weakness of work place change efforts in that program implementers are more concerned with obtaining results rather than using scientific methodology.

HEALTH PROMOTION TRENDS IN THE WORKPLACE

Most of the comprehensive programs for health promotion occur in large companies where resources are available. Proportionally, small companies have been hit just as hard, or harder by skyrocketing health care costs. A great need exists to apply the lessons learned by large companies to companies with less than 200 employees, which make up over 90% of all corporations in the U.S.

Another trend will be a greater diagnosis of organizational systems and cultural issues for evaluating the needs and readiness of a company for health promotion. Some health promotion programs have failed because of negative or adversarial relations between labor and management. Better knowledge and measurement of the cultural factors affecting health promotion is imperative. The near future also indicates a closer link between long-term cost management efforts and health promotion. Employers are beginning to realize that for any cost management effort to work in the long run, employees must ultimately play a more responsible and proactive role in their lifestyle behavior and in health care treatment choices.

A SMALL BUSINESS EXAMPLE OF HP

In 1979, in a small lumber company in Minnesota, a middle-age employee, basically in the prime of life, dropped dead of a heart attack. He was overweight, had hypertension, and exhibited a "driving" personality.

Scherer Brothers Lumber Company was a family business that witnessed the premature death of two other employees around this same time, one from a preventable yard accident and the other from suicide following a forced early retirement due to arteriosclerosis. According to Gregg Scherer, "Three good employees, three lives lost, three deaths which could have been prevented through a program of active intervention. These situations are not isolated; they happen in all corporations. When reduced to simplistic terms we were dealing with factors such as poor nutrition, lack of exercise, inability to control stress, and poor safety habits; all factors which take these tragedies out of the realm of fate and put them squarely in the arena of corporate responsibilities" *(Scherer, 1983)*.

Scherer Brothers decided to do something about their problem. The company conducted a needs assessment to determine employee interests regarding health promotion programs. The company then proceeded to create a low-cost, highly effective health promotion program based upon the following : "To create and support a healthy lifestyle and attitude, both in the workplace and at home."

Some of the supportive actions included: Removing all candy and cigarette machines from the work environment and replacing them with fruit dispensing machines; eliminating salt from all company food; and substituting decaffeinated coffee in the vending machines. In addition, programs on smoking cessation and nutrition were established. Although this was not the first small business to develop a comprehensive health promotion effort, it remains to this day one of the most successful, as well as one of the more highly visible.

This story is an excellent model for businesses everywhere. The model is actually quite simple and is based on the overwhelming recognition that health care costs are rising dramatically; poor health practices are creating great tragedies in the ranks of our workers, colleagues, and friends; and employee morale is suffering.

A FINAL WORD

Not many years ago, workplace health promotion programs were begun because they seemed like a nice benefit to provide, or were "a good idea at the time." No good data or proven formulas existed to draw from or model after. Now, employers as well as health promotion professionals know that the evidence of investing incomprehensive health promotion adds up to increased productivity through reduced costs and improved performance. We will explore some of this data in future chapters. Subsequent follow-ups of these early efforts reveal that a "win-win" outcome for organizational health promotion is possible, even predictable, when done correctly. Health promotion in the workplace can be a valuable employee benefit as well as a crucial cost containment strategy.

2

THE ORGANIZATIONAL CONTEXT: MANAGERIAL, CULTURAL AND POLICY ISSUES

INTRODUCTION

Organizations are composed of leaders, managers, power cliques, and various formal and informal alliances that can either assist or detract from the successful selection, design, or implementation of health promotion programs. The practical organizational issues that will be elaborated upon in this chapter will provide more effective strategies for ensuring successful HP programs. This chapter will also help us to answer such questions as: How can we best approach leaders, managers, contacts, and program sponsors in order to enlist their ongoing support for more successful and effective health promotion programs? What kind of organizational issues and concerns will help us to later design and effectively implement HP programs?

DEFINING THE ORGANIZATION AND HOW IT WORKS: PRINCIPLES TO KEEP IN MIND WHEN DESIGNING HP PROGRAMS

One of most important principles of any health promotion professional is that we must do our work *with* people in the entire organization, not *to* them. Getting various levels of the organization to support our health promotion is a key management issue. The issue sounds simple, but the reality is quite different.

A very simple definition of an organization is a goal-directed system in which two or more people cooperate. *Daft (1983:7)* defines organizations as " social entities that are goal directed, deliberately structured activity systems with identifiable boundaries." Organizations convert resource inputs into various outputs, products and services. Let us review the key dimensions:

1. Social entity where people and groups act together.
2. Goal directed where significant ends to pursue are chosen, whether profit or service to humanity.
3. Structure where tasks or work is divided up in some manner (division of labor) to achieve goals.
4. Coordination of activities must be coordinated to better achieve goals.
5. Continuity is required to indicate a common sense of purpose which guides the work over varying lengths of time.

The organization's vision and purpose provide continuity and direction for the goal-setting and planning processes. The budget is merely the business plan translated into financial targets for purposes of accountability. The organization's strategic direction is supported through its link with the organization's management culture (symbols, values, knowledge, styles of discourse and dress, rituals and myths, and the human resource system. The organization also exists in an environment, both internal and external, that influences strategies, tactics and policies. Many behaviors and processes such as the type of communication, conflict management, teamwork, and reward systems can either help or prevent managemen, from effectively structuring activities and processes to accomplish important organizational goals. These activities must be understood when designing health promotion programs *(Gutknecht and Miller,1986)*.

The health promotion department can have a limited budget, part-time personnel and volunteers; or it might start with a bigger budget, backed by the results of a formal and more expensive needs assessment (which would emphasize the formal goals and impacts are desired). A large health promotion department could then hire its own staff, utilize consultants, and become more sophisticated in the type and range of services and programs offered.

The HP staff will ask questions such questions as: "How can we improve the organization's bottom-line and help it meet its strategic goals by using health promotion as a tool for positive change and innovation?" Health promotion consultants can also assist in this process by clarifying issues and providing valuable expertise on topics that working staff can not possibly provide. The health promotion department focuses upon such key goals as: to change people's unhealthy and unproductive behavior into more productive behavior such as increased health awareness, positive and healthy behavioral change, or more healthy work practices and styles of interaction. All of these will have positive impacts upon organizational productivity.

The techniques used in health promotion programs are varied. They include: health risk appraisals, needs assessment, employee orientation sessions, health screenings, health workshops regarding the influence of managerial practice upon worker productivity (stress, morale, turnover); behavioral change programs aimed at mdifying the health and labor costs associated with obesity, cholesterol, poor diet, lack of exercise, high blood pressure smoking; and cultural supports, policy change and environmental modification.

WHY LEADERSHIP IS INTERESTED IN ORGANIZATIONAL HEALTH PROMOTION TODAY

Leadership is the art and science of getting things done through people. Leaders are those key individuals who must face both outward to read the signs of pivotal changes and trends around them, and then face inward to empower and energize the organization, management and all employees with vision and purpose. Leaders are the heart and blood of any organization, pumping vitality into the task and team processes and responding to the challenges that rapid change.Proactive leaders must clearly set the organizational direction and mobilize organizational resources for attaining divergent goals.

Leaders gain commitment and cooperation, move various teams or organizational units into action, and make sure that talents, skills and potentials are fully utilized. Effective leaders know how build morale through encouraging latent group talents or underutilized skills. Leaders create a climate of competence and purpose; they inspire our best efforts; they make us feel confident that we are moving in the right direction. Leaders have the power to tap into the organization's pool of experience by remaining sensitive to strategic issues, including people. Drawing upon diverse sources of information they are able to act decisively. Effective leaders revitalize both organizations and employees. Good leaders think and act proactively, which demands that they always look for creative opportunities and attempt to turn potential setbacks into a positive learning opportunities. This proactive mindset allows the organization to retain a competitive advantage. Effective leaders know how to listen, to ask questions, and identify key trends in the internal and external environment. They know that involving people is the foundation for all productive activity. When people are treated as valued assets they produce at high levels. People can do satisfactory work because they are controlled, they only achieve exceptional performance levels because they choose to identify with meaningful tasks.

It is up to good leaders to set the climate to inspire higher performance in everyone. They must create a supportive environment for risk taking and innovation. They know how important it is to enhance the quality of life for all workers. This vision of a healthy and resourceful organization places people's health and well-being on a level with other strategic considerations. Thus, managers at all levels are tasked with promoting opportunities for employee commitment by tapping into their potential for superior performance. Remember: systems don't create superior contributions, people do.

SIX THINGS ORGANIZATIONS SHOULD KNOW BEFORE BEGINNING A HEALTH PROMOTION PROGRAM
As workplace health promotion has come of age, and more comprehensive programs have appeared, a greater need exists for reliable information. The following are some guidelines for your consideration.

ONE: "Health Promotion" And "Wellness" Are More Than "Fitness." The first workplace health programs focused mainly on executive physical fitness. Companies became aware of this need when calculating the cost to replace managers due to illness or accident. Xerox has documented the cost of re-placing an executive lost to the company as a result of a heart attack: $600,000-$1,000,000. While most companies still have executive fitness pro-grams, many have expanded them to include the entire workforce, and to encompass a wider range of programs that impact the health and well-being of all employees. This is not to say that executive fitness cannot become an important component of a total program. In fact, by servicing the needs of se-nior executives, one has the opportunity to demonstrate the value of wellness activities to key decision makers who then become supporters for future pro-gram expansion to other groups in the organization.

One company looked at other areas of "wellness" after an effective mid-level manager died shortly after competing in a 10K run. This person was the outward picture of health, but an autopsy revealed blockage of the coronary arteries. This death might have been prevented through a blood pressure screening program. Depending on the assessed need of the organization, health promotion activities generally consist of a range of activities for individuals, work groups, and the entire organizationl:

- Self-Care Practices (Breast Self-Exam).
- Reduced Use of Harmful Substances (Alcohol, Drugs, and Tobacco).
- Individual Safety Practices (Seat Belt Safety, Back Injury Prevention).
- Coping Skills (Stress, Time, and Motivational Management).
- Fitness (Body Fat, Cardiovascular, Weight Control, Aerobics).
- Nutrition (Education and Intervention).
- Appropriate Use of the Health System and Health Benefits.
- Patient Compliance (Hypertension, Diabetes).
- Consumer Education (AIDS Prevention, Why Exercise or Why QuitSmoking?).
- Medical Screenings (Blood Counts, Glucose, Cholesterol)
- Workplace Policies (Smoke-Free Workplace).
- Management Education and Development.

TWO: Your Corporate Culture Will Strongly Effect Your Health Promotion Effort. A Los Angeles based savings and loan company started promoting employee health after the chief executive officer took his son to karate lessons. The CEO began working out with his son, recognized some improvements in his personal fitness, and decided to hire an expert for a similar workplace program. The activity caught on and later was expanded to other health promoting efforts.

This case is not the exception today. Employees need to feel that their leaders care about all aspects of their development, including health. This feeling is nurtured when workers from all levels of the organization take part in program planning. Those programs that begin health promotion without proper input and planning usually die due to lack of participation. There is little doubt that it is the support of top leadership and organizational culture that provides the foundation for eventual success.

The term, corporate culture, is used to describe how the company operates on all levels: What do managers and workers say about working conditions? How do employees relate to each other? Does the company provide a positive climate for personal growth and career development? These and many other issues establish the culture of an organization. A positive corporate culture can assist in creating strong health promotion programs, and it may also help to establish and solidify an emergent concern by organizational leaders regarding the need for improved productivity by investing in people. We will pursue this topic in more depth in a latter section of this chapter.

THREE: Know Your Company's True Health Care Costs And Trends. Do you know how much your company is spending for the health, illness, and accidents of your employees? If your company is average, you are probably paying around $2,600 per employee just for medical insurance (1986). The estimates of costs for the average smoker to the organization ranges from $350 to $750 per employee and $3,000 to 5,000 per smoker. Each company may absorb as much as $1,000 in health costs per overweight employee. Before beginning a wellness program, you should know the company's history of health costs, including some estimated standards for comparing health costs in problem areas, and data trends comparing the organization with its industry norms. For instance, annual increases in health care premiums are currently running significantly above the inflation rate while other health cost areas are also increasing. All of following health categories are potential candidates for cost containment efforts:

1. Turnover for Medical Reasons.
2. Paid Sick Leave.
3. Unpaid Sick Leave.
4. Medical Disability, Retirement for Medical Reasons, and Disability Insurance.
5. Medical Related Lawsuits.
6. Group Health Insurance, Health Maintenance Organizations (HMOs), and

Preferred Provider Organizations (PPOs), Dental, and other group health plans.

7. Workers' Compensation.
8. Rehabilitation Programs
9. Utilization Management Fees.
10. Employee Assistance Program.
11. Health Promotion.
12. Administration.

Companies cannot afford to ignore the cost of employee health. Incredibly, many are now paying around $5,500 to $6,500 per employee. Of even greater concern, at the present rate of increase, within five years these same companies will pay even higher amounts. The systematic efforts to contain these costs include three strategies:

1. Redesigning the benefits package.
2. Providing alternative medical delivery systems for employees (HMOs, PPOs).
3. Promoting health in the workplace.

We will explore the impact of this third strategy, health promotion, on the reduction of cost escalation throughout this text.

FOUR: Health Promotion Programs Cut Health Care Costs When Developed And Implemented Correctly. The most common reasons that health promotion efforts fail are deficiencies that are inherent in the initial design of the program. They are:

1. A lack of upper management support.
2. A lack of clear identification of goals.
3. Poor planning.
4. A lack of employee participation, which usually results from some combination of the first three.

When a program succeeds, the "payoffs" can be documented in a number of important ways. An improved employee-employer relationship and a good public image are two that can not easily or quickly be measured quantitatively. But what are companies reporting on the cost savings side of this issue? In general, the answer is very positive even though one or two years is usually not long enough to see substantial results. Employees must practice new lifestyle behaviors for sustained periods of at least three to five years before decreases can be seen in health care utilization. However, once they begin to understand that certain symptoms do not just mean disease, then absentee-ism and turnover may decrease due to a perception of an improved organiza-tional climate and quality of life. The following are some excellent companies that are enjoying cost savings through health promotion efforts *(Gutknecht and Gutknecht,1988)*:

Control Data--Extensive evaluation of their "Staywell" program has shown numerous positive results. Overall, the percentage of employees who smoke has declined 35% in 1980 to 26% in 1986; the percentage of overweight has dropped from 27% for participants and 36% for non-participants. The annual savings in health care claims and absenteeism due to risk reduction is $1.8 million. This company is receiving a return-on-dollar invested ratio of about 2-to-1!

Johnson & Johnson--An analysis of their "Live For Life" program over a 5-year period showed that employees who did not participate in the program spent twice as much annually on in-patient hospital care as those who took part.

AT&T--The "Total Life Concept" program five-year results show that reduction or elimination of certain types of illnesses among employees has resulted in $4.8 million for medical sav-ings and $31.2 million total projected savings per year per 100,000 employees, while costing the company $2.2 million per year. Also, based upon reduction in risk for 100,000 employees, the number of cancers has declined 240 and number of heart attacks has declined 1,481. Their estimates for costs of a heart attack or stroke range from $250,000 to $1 million per case, de-pending on age, income, pre- and post-productivity loss, replacement cost, retraining costs, and salary continuation.

Blue Cross/Blue Shield of Indiana--The "Stay Alive and Well" program for their own employees resulted in savings of $1.65 million in the four years 1978-1982, as measured by reduced rates of absenteeism and employee insurance claims. Overall, the participants averaged $ 519 less in insurance bene-fits spent per participant and savings of $143 per employee over a 5 year period for 2,411 employees.

Madison, Wisconsin Teachers Association--A balanced program of exercise, good nutrition, and stress management reduced absenteeism by 17%.

New York Telephone--Began a nine-component program that included smoking cessation, hypertension control, fitness training, stress management, alcohol abuse control, colon and breast cancer screening, and a low-back disability prevention program. Savings relative to cost were 2-to-1.

Southern Bell--Improved safety at the work site, coupled with preventive health services for the work force, led to significant savings in medical care and disability costs. They reduced disability costs for each $1,000 of total wage payments from $13.28 to $9.43 in a recent 2-year period. These savings are expected to increase even in the face of inflationary wage costs.

Some additional Data--two studies reported in *The American Journal of Health Promotion (1987)* confirm some of these findings: In the first study, participants in a work site health promotion program averaged 24% lower health care costs than nonparticipants. The five-year reduction in health care costs relative to savings per employee was $45 per year ($143.60 savings less $98.86 costs). Health care costs for exercisers were $339 compared to $596 for non-exercisers. In the second study cited, participants in a hypertension and stress control program decreased their annual mean health care claim from $225 to $85, a reduction of 62.25%. This last study is often cited as one of the best controlled studies of health promotion programs.

PROFILE OF A MULTI-COMPONENT HP PROGRAM

Control Data Company of Minneapolis, Minnesota, began their *StayWell* program in 1977, and several components were initially piloted in 1979. Phased implementation to Control Data work sites began in 1980. By the end of 1985 the *StayWell* program had been implemented in most major U.S. work sites, and the program is currently available to over 70% of Control Data's full time U.S. employees. *StayWell* has undergone tremendous evolution since its beginning in 1979. Much of this evolution has been the direct result of evaluation of pilot materials and processes that identified program strengths and weaknesses. The relatively "mature" program of today includes many interrelated components listed below.

1. **Employee Health Survey**--Assists in organizational health needs assessment, program planning and evaluation.

2. **Pre-Implementation Site Planning--**This prepares the work site personnel and key management for successful implementation.

3. **Orientation Session--**Explains the program to prospective participants and invites them to enroll.

4. **Health Risk Assessment--**Screens employees for major risk factors.

5. **Interpretation Session--**Explains Health Risk Assessment results and encourages participation in StayWell educational and action components.

6. **Lifestyle Change Courses--**Programs are offered in three different delivery modes: instructor led, self-study and computer based.

7. **Health Campaigns--**Brings an intensive focus on a particular health promotion concern, incorporates incentives and evaluation instruments.

8. **Action Teams--**These are on-going employee-led groups focused on specific wellness activities or work site issues.

9. *WellTimes--*A quarterly wellness news magazine for employees and their families.

10. **Special Events--**Periodic promotions highlighting specific wellness concerns.

FIVE: Workers Who Are Practicing a "Wellness" Lifestyle Will Not Benefit as Much as Those Who are Not. A Southern California company was elated when they first found that employees participating in their on-site aerobic exercise class had significantly fewer health claims than those who did not. This seemed to justify the program's existence until further analysis revealed a "self-selection" process that is a fact-of-life for most workplace health promotion programs: The workers who were exercising on-site were the same ones who would be doing so anyway. This phenomenon, known as "The Healthy Worker Effect," is not an argument against workplace programs. Your program is best served when you have these people acting as enthusiastic and supporting role models for the rest of your workforce. However, awareness of this fact can help you plan marketing and promotion of your program to those groups who are harder to reach and who are usually at higher risk for illness and injury. Typically, the "healthy actives" will represent about 10-20% of the total workforce. The continuum below illustrates an approximate breakdown of employee attitudes toward health promotion *(Gutknecht and Gutknecht,1988)*.

EMPLOYEE WELLNESS ATTITUDE CONTINUUM

[D=20%   ] [C=30%   ] [B=30%   ] [A=20%   ]
>>>

A = Active employees: currently pursuing a wellness life-style.

B = Borderline employees: need help in getting started, but many have the potential to become Actives.

C = Contented employees: satisfied with present lifestyle, and need to be convinced that wellness is beneficial to them or worth their pursuit.

D = Doubters: employees who may never participate short of a major health event.

All workforces vary in these percentages depending on industry and other organizational variables, but the goal remains the same: Move employees in all groups as far to the right as possible toward active participation. To accomplish this, you must meet the most important challenge facing health promotion professionals, according to health educator Don Ardell, "reaching those who have the greatest need."

SIX: How You Promote Your Program Will Greatly Influence Participation. How well you promote will not only affect participation, it will probably determine whether your program survives. The following are a few program development and promotion tips that might help your health promotion efforts. This topic is also covered in chapter seven.

1. Your employees will see health promotion as a valuable fringe benefit if it is presented to them in the right way. We have heard managers say, "We polled our people and they don't seem to want a wellness program." While participation is generally voluntary, you must apply good principles of promotion and marketing to your programs. The same principles apply to health promotion consultants who want to market their health promotion programs; presentations must be credible and persuasive. All levels of the organization must get the message through persuasive communication, innovative motivation and meaningful incentives.

2. Do not assume that you know what health promotion programs your employees need and want until you ask them or survey their needs and interests. Not only must you ask them, you should do so in a way that effectively brings them into the planning process. Once again the principles of effective communication will stimulate involvement, active participation, and help the processgain acceptance.

3. Do not assume that you know what is right for your employees. Many well-intentioned leaders, managers, and health promotion consultants have started programs and failed because they were certain they knew the health, or other problems of the workforce without assessing the situation. As above, the best policy is always to explore the the needs and interests of your workers first; ask your workers about their preferred health promotion activities and always include them in the planning process.

4. Know your company's demographics. You would not provide the same exercise options to a young, female-dominated workforce that you would to middle-age male workers. Age and sex differences may be obvious, but other demographics are not. The health promotion coordinator or planner can get help from managers with marketing backgrounds to help others identify and understand the concepts of segmented target markets (subpopulations of workers, their attitudes, values and interests), identify which health behaviors might negatively impact their work performance, and hence require viable alternative behaviors. This information is also very useful when designing behavioral change workshops.

5. Speak the language of your workforce. Use some of the same savvy you might use to promote and market your company's products or services. Do not invite your workers to attend a "Health Risk Appraisal" if they have no idea what one is. Explain it clearly and sell it first. You might consider a brochure or flyer (complete with a cartoon) that captures their attention with visual appeal and uses everyday words understood by everyone.

IMPACTS OF ORGANIZATIONAL CULTURE

The daily lives of our employees are intimately tied and shaped by culture. But what do we really mean by this assertion? Culture permeates our perception of work relations below the level of our conscious awareness; it molds our view of the way we feel about working at this place. Culture is that layer of organizational meaning and purpose that leaders and managers need to become familiar wit, because they can not renew the health and productivity of their organization without addressing it. Let us first define organizational or corporate culture through its components which are myths, rituals, stories, sagas, ceremony, humor, symbols, values and language. *Cohen et al (1980:337),* expands this definition:

> The customary way of doing things, attitude values that are 'in the air' affecting every one. The organization's attitude about authority, how it should be used, interpersonal style, conflicts and so forth, which condition and affect all other changes.

Each organization has its own unique culture or way of doing things. Just like the larger society, it also has groups that produce divergent values and standards of appropriateness. Leadership is often faced with the task of turning this diversity to the organization's advantage. No organization functions without diverse values in a state of tension. This is why goal agreement, much less attainment, is not a simple process.

UNDERSTANDING THE IMPACT OF ORGANIZATIONAL CULTURE UPON HEALTH AND PRODUCTIVITY

Reactive and ineffective leadership often ignores the issue of managing culture and its relationship to health and productivity. *Deal and Kennedy (1982:16)* recommend promoting a strong organizational culture because it is healthy. A healthy culture supports the search for development programs that make people more effective and productive.

People feel better about what they do when they do things well. Working smarter is a sign of a healthy organizational culture. Strong culture companies remove a great deal of uncertainty from the environment because they provide constant and clear guidelines for effective and productive behavior. This impacts the quality of work life, and certainly health. Such a strong culture is often embodied in its daily leadership, management philosophy, and style. Cultural values also support the connection that management style has upon health and productivity. This process is accomplished through the competent human relations skills of managers who are rewarded themselves for understanding the impact that their style of interaction and communication has upon worker health and productivity. The benefits of bringing this clarity of purpose into line management philosophy to promote health and productivity is best described by *Albert and Silverman (1984: 13)* who suggest the following results:

1. Greater commitment to the organization's objectives, notably quality, good customer service, and high productivity.
2. Increased employee effort, pride and loyalty.
3. Lower turnover.
4. Faster implementation of plans, projects, and programs.
5. More effective problem solving at all organizational levels.
6. The ability to grow rapidly through directing more effort towards implementing plans, programs and objectives, and less effort towards fighting fires, plugging holes, and constantly resolving conflicts about how things should be done around here.

Understanding the cultural context is crucial for assessing the meaning of managerial performance and organizational effectiveness. Cultural issues help the organization to better perceive how to promote healthier workers and to design more effective work structures; how to obtain resources/assistance; how to gain credibility; and finally, how the organization views health promotion as a possible productivity enhancing option.

ALIGNING THE HP SYSTEM WITH THE ORGANIZATION'S CULTURAL SYSTEM

Culture influences our daily work behavior. A healthy work culture supports a strong climate for positive interaction and sustains our commitment to wellness, reasonable stress levels (moderate) and innovation. Unhealthy work cultures support a negative environment of failure, characterized by low morale, poor health and well-being, high levels of stress, absenteeism, turnover, and low productivity. The productive organization supports healthy, positive and functional cultural values and norms. Thus, changing and eliminating negative cultural norms is necessary for making organizational culture compatible with both organizational and personal productivity. By examining the cultural system we can ask better questions about the strengths and weaknesses of a particular organization in order to better identify possible barriers to the implementation of successful health promotion programs.

In order to design a good HP program, we must know the key problems, belief systems and other cultural obstacles we face. The HP consultant or department must determine how the organization perceives itself, its problems, the formal and informal pathways for seeking needed commitment and assistance, and the level of innovation or change necessary for minimal impact. These are tasks for cultural analysis.

CULTURAL ANALYSIS USING ORGANIZATIONAL NORMS

Refer to the following positive norms to understand what will support or hinder your HP efforts:

1. **Norms of positive organizational and personal pride**--people support traditions of high performance and excellence and enjoy seeing othres excel.

2. **Norms of positive performance and excellence**--people always try to improve, even when doing well.

3. **Norms of teamwork and communication**--people are good listeners and actively seek out good ideas and opinions.

4. **Norms of leadership**--all our leaders really care about making the organization an excellent and still caring place to work and model these norms in all encounters.

5. **Norms of profitability and cost-effectiveness**--people evaluate their expenditures at all levels and analyze their impact upon the bottom line and competent performance. Waste and employee theft are seldom major problems.

6. **Norms of group/team/unit relations**-- people work well in teams, are able to subordinate their egos when important for group effectiveness and refuse to take advantage of others.

7. **Norms of customer/client relations**--people are constantly looking for better ways to serve their clients or customers. However, they always treat each other just as well as they treat customers.

8. **Norms of honesty and truthfulness**--people are honest and truthful. This allows good feedback and is the foundation for open communication, worker dignity and a good measure of self-government.

9. **Norms of training and development**--people believe that the organization really supports the opportunity for better training, development and work related growth.

10. **Norms of innovation and change**--people are constantly on the lookout for the impacts of change, and are responsive to trends and the possibilities of better ways of doing things.

At the behavioral level you may focus upon the following questions which will assist you (as programs are set up) to determine how seriously the organization supports the health promotion effort and behavioral change:

1. Is positive health behavior and involvement in setting up the health promotion system and programs being rewarded or penalized by the organization and in what ways?

2. Is this behavior being visibly modeled by leaders of the organization?

3. Are people receiving feedback and information relating to whether they are effectively practicing their new health behaviors ?

4. Are the day-to-day actions and interactions supportive of this behavior?

5. Does the training and management development system support this behavior and other supporting skills in connection with it?

6. How is the behavior supported in group activities and practices?

7. Are time and other valued resources allocated in ways that support this new wellness behavior?

Some additional techniques for understanding cultural issues that might help you to improve your information about the organization and build a more successful program are as follows:

1. Do not be thrown off by unexpected rejection by some mangers who might even poke fun at your efforts. Establish your perspective to assist the organization become more effective in all dimensions, keep a good sense of humor and allow yourself to be surprised by interesting facts and revelations. Try to always get a good feel for those people who may prove to be your biggest supporters and accept all offers from those willing to lend expertise or resources.

2. Be systematic when observing and checking reported facts or the observations of others. Are these patterned and repeated facts/experiences or merely idiosyncratic events? Check often where people in authority have a strong desire to make an impact.

3. Locate knowledgeable managers, supporters and resource people from all sectors of the organization. Involve the people who you are using as assistants, observers and information sources as future designers, planners, supporters and participants of your health promotion efforts.

4.   Reveal your findings and questions to everyone possible. Try to get them to explain what is going on, and contradictions between negative and positive cultural items (myths, values, rituals, ceremonies). Also, where good information (whatever its uses) and customer satisfaction are essential, then try to get the real facts.

5.   Formalize your ideas about which norms support positive actions.Systematically check and consolidate information and hunches.

6.   Go over the history of the organization, when it was founded, who were the founders, what were their values and any important events in the past, and most recent past. What have been the most recent problems that might have some relationship to productivity and health cost issues? Do they have anything to do with issues related to other costs, morale, stress, corporate image, negative practices like theft, absenteeism, turnover, and lack of loyalty? What are some of the critical incidents that seem to indicate concern or disregard for employees and their health concerns?

This cultural perspective is built upon the assumption that by first studying positive and productive work cultural values, norms and behaviors, then we can nurture those that support more effective health production programs. Organizational culture can also negatively impact the management system and other systems essential for building successful HP programs. We need to know those areas that might become obstacles to our best efforts. We must educate potentially supportive managers about the impacts that these negative norms have on the success of their organization.

Think about the positive and negative norms in your organization (or one that you would like to work with) and which ones might add or detract from an effective HP effort. How would you change the negative norms and behaviors as a consultant? What norms could employees change themselves? How have these negative norms impacted health, personal habits, or work behavior in the organization?

THE CHALLENGE OF CREATING HEALTHY WORK SYSTEMS
The healthy organization should be our ultimate goal. By promoting this vision, we will help establish a framework for increasing both personal and organizational productivity and effectiveness. It will also assist us to attend to

- All health problems can be broken down into component pieces and solved independently of each other, as long as we use rational and logical problem-solving methods.

- It's all right to blame our failures on those other individuals and trends beyond our control. Let's think of ourselves as machines who work without any need for preventive maintenance and find ways to shift responsibility for our poor health and productivity.

- Let fear of risk taking dominate and make sure to display surprise when we hear that our best executive have had heart attacks.

- Adopt a philosophy which views health, wellness and even innovation as taking abrupt and drastic risks that we cannot afford to gamble upon. Thus, any strategy that we adopt needs to show immediate results and instant successes. Small improvements in the short-run, prove nothing.

In contrast, proactive assumptions suggest more healthy and dynamic possibilities that are applicable at any level of personal behavior or organizational effectiveness:

- Anticipate unhealthy issues and concerns before they become costly problems, erupt into crisis or overwhelm our abilities to respond effectively, "attend to it constantly, even before it breaks."

- All problems can not be reduced to logical pieces of a puzzle and solved independently of each other. Both the human body and organizations are interdependent systems whose parts work best when in a state of healthy balance.

- Take responsibility for your own health, anticipate and examine behaviors, values and trends which might negatively impact your effectiveness or your company's productivity now and in the future.

- Face fear and resistance to innovative programs, like health promotion, by embracing moderate risk. Do not let yourself ignore those signals which indicate that some thing is even slightly wrong, even when it appears to most people that everything is perfectly all right.

- Adopt a philosophy which views success, wellness and productive living as an integrated, and gradual process of improvement; practical outcomes that must slowly be built upon a solid, long-term foundation.

The signals are becoming clearer everyday that the old assumptions are dying and new, more creative responses are demanded. The challenge ahead is that we involve all our workers in order to utilize their most innovative capabilities for designing healthy organizations.

Leaders and managers must learn to create a healthy climate that encourages more adaptable, creative and productive work environments. To get productive results we need to support programs--including health promotion and human resource development--that assist workers to increase their health, energy and vitality through leading more balanced and resourceful lives. Managers and leaders can begin by improving their own health, wellness and energy. Armed with a personal commitment to their own wellness lifestyle, workers will see the benefits that effective managers themselves model each day.

Those who desire to develop, administer or consult in health promotion programs must be able to effectively bring together appropriate resources to get the organization excited about the many benefits of health promotion. This person needs to be both practical and resourceful, and should be able to strategically sell the advantages of various health promotion options. They must provide the cohesion and direction for temporary teams, planning groups, committees, marketing and promotion efforts and program execution. One of the more important requisites of this challenging role will be the skill for working with people, rather than for them.

HEALTH PROMOTION POLICY QUESTIONS

The final issue of this chapter concerns the issue of organizational policy. In order to support our definition of health promotion that includes improving information, awareness and behavioral outcomes, we need to provide environmental and policy supports for these changes. Some examples of policy changes included in a seat-belt program for all those employees driving company cars might include, communicated disciplinary measures for noncompliance, instructions for supervisor's responsibility to monitor and enforce the program requirements and a short-lived campaign to kick off the policy. Other areas of health promotion that might utilize policy to help sustain more successful health promotion programs include:

1. Smoke-free workplace. (Example #1).
2. Employee Assistance Programs (intervening before existing problem affects work performance to the point of dismissal).
3. Incentive and reward systems for healthy behaviors.
4. Air quality control.
5. Personnel policies (sick leave, etc.).
6. Healthy food programs.

EXAMPLE OF POLICY FOR A SMOKE-FREE WORKPLACE

Q. What are the benefits of a Smoking Controlled Environment?

A. Smoke-control measures are yielding human resource dividends to organizations from four primary sources: Health and safety, employee morale, productivity and corporate image. The benefits discussed in the next section can be applied to most health promotion programs, with some variation for specific program impacts.

Health and Safety--High on the list of pluses that accrue to a smoke-free organization is the knowledge that a positive step has been taken to remove the primary source of indoor air pollution. Health and safety issues are a major concern today among employees and employee bargaining units. No single step will go as far toward asserting an organization's commitment to health and safety than to implement a policy which removes ambient tobacco smoke from the workplace.

Employee Morale--Another benefit from smoking control is enhanced employee morale. Contrary to the fears of many personnel managers, employees overwhelmingly favor the elimination of smoking from their own work areas. Surveys conducted in recent years by companies like Pacific Telephone and Pacific Northwest Bell show that nearly nine out of ten nonsmokers and over half of the smokers want smoking strictly controlled or banned from their workplaces. Nearly three out of four employees who work indoors are nonsmokers. These statistics indicate that about 80% of all indoor workers desire a restricted smoking environment. Companies that have already banned smoking, or have at least moved it away from work stations and into smoking lounges, are pointing to increased morale as one of the most significant, albeit unexpected, benefits from their smoke-free policies.

Productivity--Another unexpected benefit has been increased productivity from reduced costs. Consider the following examples:

Unigard Insurance implemented a work-station smoking ban three years ago and its outside cleaning service gave the company an unsolicited $500 reduction in its monthly cleaning bill.

The Austad Company in Sioux Falls self-insures for the first $15,000 of health coverage for each of its smoke-free employees. A smoke-free workforce will use the health-care system at only a fraction of the level demanded by an organization that employs smokers. Austad's cost of providing complete health coverage amounts to approximately one-third of what a comparable organization pays for the same coverage.

Radar Electric in Seattle reduced its routine maintenance budget by just over $25,000 per year once it banned smoking and stopped hiring smokers--which worked out to about $750 per year for every smoker on the payroll at the time the policy was implemented.

The Hill Air Force Base Hazard Report estimates that a smoking ban could save the Air Force over $30 million per year at Hill AFB alone, $1.3 billion Air Force wide, and $4.3 billion in all facilities operated by the U.S. Department of Defense.

Boeing Company's former medical director estimated that Boeing will save over $10 million in the first year of its announced total ban on smoking throughout the company's premises.

Weyerhaeuser Corporation recently studied the cost of smoking in its corporate headquarters. In an interoffice communication, the company concluded, "we estimate smoking costs at corporate headquarters to be $4.9 million annually."

Organizations that adopt strong smoking-control measures can expect to save dollars from reduced insurance premiums for employee life, disability, industrial accident and health policies, as well as from negotiated discounts on fire insurance. In the long term, the company will save from substantially reduced rates of employee absenteeism, working age mortality and early retirement. Smokers, on the average, are absent from work twice as often as nonsmokers, and their rates of mortality and disability are up to seven times greater at certain age intervals, within the normal work life.

Corporate Image--Finally, some organizations, especially those in the professional service sector, perceive a benefit to corporate image from restricting smoking among their employees. Many accounting and law firms for example, proscribe smoking for all professional personnel when they are working--whether on client premises, in their own offices, or anywhere when they are representing the firm. The reasons for the policies have little to do with concern for health or safety--they have to do with professionalism. In many professional environments smoking is no longer considered an appropriate behavior.

LEGAL ISSUES IN WORKPLACE SMOKING CONTROL

Ironically, when the topic of workplace smoking is raised, questions concerning "smokers' rights" and the legality of implementing smoking bans tend to predominate. This is a misplaced emphasis. The legal risk facing American businesses from the so-called smoking issue stems entirely from failure to take effective measures to protect employees from exposure to ambient smoke in the workplace--not from taking those steps. The following discussion addresses the most commonly raised legal concerns.

Q. Is it possible to severely restrict or even totally ban smoking in the workplace?
A. The answer is an emphatic yes! The right of an employer to make and enforce reasonable rules of conduct on its premises is protected by the laws of every labor agreement. Restrictions against smoking, if written and implemented properly, would be deemed reasonable in every jurisdiction in this country. Employers routinely impose similar behavioral constraints against singing, playing radios, harassing co-workers, loitering and other actions that interfere with the work flow or irritate fellow employees. Smoking is both an irritant and a health hazard to other employees.

Q. What about the rights of smokers?
A. This is a red herring. Smokers enjoy the same rights in and out of the workplace as do nonsmokers. "Smokers' rights" are not threatened by a smoking ban. There simply is no "right to smoke" on the job. Put simply, the right to smoke at work is not one of the many smokers' rights, any more than is the right to sing at work for the singer, or to whistle at work for the whistler, or to drink at work for the drinker.

Q. Is a policy which restricts hiring to nonsmokers discriminatory?

A. Yes. So are all policies which prescribe applicant qualifications or impose behavioral standards based on achieved personal attributes. Employers regularly and unabashedly discriminate in hiring on the basis of prior work experience, academic credentials, willingness to relocate, attention to personal grooming and acceptance of reasonable work rules. Smoking is an acquired behavior--not an ascribed characteristic like race, sex, or national origin--and it is not one of the protected behaviors under our civil rights laws (nor will it become one).

Some employers are now openly restricting hiring consideration to non-smokers; many others are doing so covertly. Employers are taking this extra step in order to guarantee long term success for their clean-air policies. They are not trying to be Draconian, only realistic. They recognize that smoking is a powerful drug addiction and that withdrawal from nicotine can be a wrenching experience for those who are tobacco dependent. Restricting hiring to applicants who are comfortable describing themselves as "nonsmokers" on a job application accomplishes two things:

1. It secures a formal acknowledgement and acceptance of the company's smoke-free policy by every new employee.

2. It limits hiring to individuals who feel they can function during an eight- or nine-hour period without smoking--i.e., to applicants who are either nonsmokers, very light smokers, or smokers who have made a personal commitment to quitting.

Q. What are some possible ramifications if we do not control smoking in the workplace?

A. Finally we come to the real liability issue. Health economists believe that virtually every responsible business organization in this country will be enforcing strict smoking control before the end of this decade. The reason is health and safety liability. Research on the health effects from passive smoking--breathing someone else's discarded tobacco smoke--is becoming legion. There is no longer doubt among those who have examined the research that passive smoking is an immediate health risk for those who are afflicted with pulmonary and cardiovascular disorders, and a serious, long-term risk for everyone else. In *1983, the American Medical Association* concluded that, "research during the last decade has yielded steadily accumulating evidence indicting tobacco smoke as a significant health hazard to the nonsmoker." Since then many researchers, including the *Surgeon General*, have reconfirmed the relationship between passive smoking and illness and death; the Environmental Protection Agency implicated passive smoking as the cause of between 500 and 5,000 cancer deaths per year.

Q. What will happen if we do not ban smoking on the job?
A. Your company will likely join a growing list of organizations that have been sued by employees who claim health damage from exposure to smoke in the workplace, organizations like New Jersey Bell Telephone, Western Electric, the Veterans Administration, Transworld Airlines, and the Merit Systems Protection Board (U.S. Government). And, if these recent court decisions are predictive, the litigants will be successful if your organization has not taken effective steps to protect them from involuntary exposure to tobacco smoke.

In summary, there are no legal barriers to implementing strict smoking control, to banning all smoking on company property or to restricting hiring to nonsmokers. On the other hand, there is significant legal and economic risk facing every organization which continues to expose employees to a toxic pollutant that can readily be removed by a simple, reasonable work rule.

BECOMING A SMOKE-FREE ORGANIZATION

There are as many successful strategies for moving toward a smoke-free work environment as there are methods for quitting smoking. And, as with quitting smoking, it is not so much the method that brings success as it is the determination to succeed.

Resolve to Clean the Air--Just as a smoker must resolve unconditionally to become a former smoker, an organization must resolve unconditionally to become smoke-free. If there is one generalization that could be made about approaches and policies that have met with less than optimal success, it is that the organization's goal was compromised. Instead of searching for means and methods for achieving the smoke-free objective, the organization that becomes mired in searching for exceptions will ultimately thwart that objective. For example, one well-known bank recently implemented a policy to ban smoking from all work stations, except private offices. Perhaps the bank's primary objective was to inspire smokers to achieve rapid promotion to private office status, rather than to clean the air? That kind of insensitive approach creates a sort of workplace struggle between smokers who can and those who can not. And, of course, it does little to ensure indoor air quality since most office ventilation systems recirculate the ambient smoke from private offices to surrounding offices so that everyone can enjoy it.

Decentralized Failure--Perhaps the worst-case example of a policy which offends everyone--smokers and nonsmokers alike--is also one of the most common that meekly-managed organizations offer as a way to deal with the "smoking problem." It has variations, but in each case involves letting the decision about smoking be made separately by employee units or areas within the company. For instance, employees in purchasing decide among themselves whether to permit smoking, as do employees in general accounting, employees in personnel, and so forth. Some of the company's workers, usually those whose supervisors are non-smokers, enjoy reasonably clean air, and the rest suffer quietly in order not to offend the boss. The air circulation system at least guarantees some degree of fairness by spreading the smoke around. This approach was tried at Pacific Northwest Bell, where, according to a survey of employees, approximately 80% of the workforce wanted to work in clean air. The policy enjoyed almost universal dissatisfaction. Now they are entirely smoke-free and satisfaction is high.

Employee Participation--Employee involvement from the outset is the best approach to assure both that the eventual policy will be a strong one that will gain widespread support among employees. If you are concerned that a participative approach might lead to a policy which is too weak and ineffective, your worries are unfounded. Experience indicates that group dynamics will move the policy toward more, rather than less, severity. With most workforces comprising at least two or more nonsmokers for every smoker, most employee task forces will begin working on the problem with members assuming moderate views as to how the policy should be formulated. As the group further studies and deliberates on the policy design task, it will begin moving toward a progressively more restrictive policy. Complete workplace bans are a common outcome of this group approach.

Timeline--Most organizations recognize that eliminating smoking from the workplace constitutes a major change in the workplace culture, a major change made more complex because of the attendant problems related to drug addiction.

This is not to say that a company must look to a long-term arduous transition period to move from where it is to becoming smoke-free. Boyd Coffee in Portland implemented its smoking ban by posting a notice on Friday that smoking would no longer be allowed, effective on Monday. The policy has been successful since its inception twelve years ago. But most employers see a transitional period as a more sensitive human resource type response, which is ultimately a more successful route to corporate clean air. Group Health Cooperative of Puget Sound, for example, one of the largest employers in the State of Washington, hired an independent consultant to plan and direct the implementation of its smoke-free program. The phase-in period lasted approximately ten months. This transition period is not uncommon in large companies, but beyond this point companiesmay be perceived as being unsure of how to proceed, or incompetent and mean spirited.

During the transition period, and continuing thereafter, most organizations offer help to smokers who want to stop smoking.The cost of proprietary cessation programs are often shared or paid for in full by the employer and in most cases, cessation programs are conducted on the company's premises. Pegging cost reimbursement to success is sometimes used as an additional incentive. But the strongest cessation incentive is the company's commitment to a smoke-free work environment; smoking rates among employees in smoke-free organizations drop rapidly to negligible levels:

> The rate at Radar Electric went from 50% to one percent within three years after the policy took force. Riviera Motors in Portland expected its smoking rate to be at five percent by 1984 (it had dropped from 35% to 15% by 1981, two years into the policy). Northern Life Insurance, which stopped hiring smokers in November of 1983, expects to be totally smoke-free within a few years.

Please see chapter 6 for a more in-depth discussion of a specific program for helping workers to quit smoking. But for now let us turn to the topic of behavioral change.

3

MANAGING BEHAVIORAL CHANGE

INTRODUCTION

This chapter explores the skillsfor effectively managing behavioral change. We are in a major change in the way that we perceive both health and its meaning in the wider context of organizational and cultural values.These values are central to patient's identities and their ability to make significant behavioral changes. We must find new ways to bridge the gap between appropriate health behaviors, treatment practices, and the cultural and support structures that can help us to transform the entire environment of poor health.This is a very complex process and the difficulties should not be iunderestimated.

Organizational health promotion is a strategic effort to reduce the health risks of employees through planned changes in individual risk related behaviors and other organizationally related predisposing conditions. Organizational health promotion, thus, focuses upon changes in both individuals and organizations in order to reduce health risks. This proactive and preventive approach provides both the motivational and environmental supports that encourage individuals to examine their behaviors, to decide what they need to change and how to change it. These support systems can have a profound effect upon worker's self-esteem, and influence whether or not individuals choose to participate.

The group nature of the modern workplace can be utilized to help individuals to become more motivated to make effective decisions about changing their poor health and work habits. In fact, several researchers have noted that when we rely solely upon behavior change, and fail to provide intervention and support, the success of programs is less substantial.

As we stated earlier in chapter 2, program success may be attributed to factors beyond health improvements brought about by behavioral change. Some of the more important factors are increased organizational awareness of general health and utilization issues, changes in work culture and job design, improved management practices, policy changes and the appreciation of employees. Thus, health promotion, like good human resource development programs, must focus upon various levels of intervention that stimulate, motivate and inspire workers and organizations to change. Let us go back to the basics once again to review the process leading up to the behavioral change workshops.

HEALTH PROMOTION AND LEVELS OF BEHAVIORAL CHANGE
In chapter one we discussed the three levels of organizational health promotion. Here, let us briefly discuss a slightly different view of these stages as they apply to behavioral change.

1. Awareness and Information
The first level is focused upon creating awareness by providing information through introductory talks about health promotion or payroll stuffers on changing negative health behaviors. This level is concerned with general health information, along with structured assessment programs, i.e., hypertension control screenings and Health Risk Appraisals (HRA). These programs serve to determine risk factors which predispose disease. This feedback begins to consolidate some of the information gained through awareness and utilize it to assess and make later behavioral change more relevant and likely.

2. Behavioral change programs
The second level is composed of fairly comprehensive health promotion programs that focus upon ongoing behavioral change. These programs include workshops on a variety of specific health and wellness topics such

as smoking cessation, cholesterol and high-blood pressure control and, weight or stress reduction. This level also includes opportunities for promoting personal development through human resource incentives, rewards and supporting policies. We are also trying to help each individual begin to change those unproductive behaviors over which they can exert some control, whether work or lifestyle.

3. Organizational Change Impacts Upon Behavioral change

This level contains programs that address the full range of structural and leadership issues. The topics of concern are organizational work redesign, cultural change, organizational philosophy, values, norms, and management styles. Any training program or program for behavioral change can build upon this information. We can also observe that personal development can be encouraged and supported by organizational actions, policies, and changes.

For example, a person gains information and makes self-assessments through participating in company-sponsored programs, then makes decisions about personal plans for change (with the assistance of organizational policies, incentives, and rewards), and finally, takes action (supported by the organizational culture and structure). Personal changes that are not supported by the organizational culture and comprehensive programs are not likely to be long lasting.

WELLNESS AND CHANGE

We live in an age of rapid change, increasing international competition, new trends and fads, and an epidemic of mergers, cutbacks and takeovers. We might call this the *era of the three C's: accelerating Change, increasing Complexity, and intensifying Competition.* Today is also a time of discontinuity, turbulence, and unpredictable events which create great challenges for managers and promoters of health and wellness. Yesterday's thinking, values and skill development have become increasingly obsolete in a world where constant transformation is the standard, not the exception. Such a situation requires our most creative thinking about changing unhealthy and unproductive behavior.

The promotion of organizational health is necessary in a world of rapid-paced changes. In fact, it is essential to examine our beliefs, behaviors and habits. Mastering such assessment and life-style change skills is part of an active learning strategy, which Dunn calls *adaptation,* and whichwe label, *behavioral flexibility.* This responsiveness to changing our un-healthy behaviors can only occur if we proceed more systematically than we have in the past.

One set of strategies for those concerned with the promotion of individual and organizational wellness is promoting programs that support healthy changes in: bad personal habits; unhealthy interpersonal relationships; poorly managed work relations and structures; ineffective personal and organizational performance; destructive organizational and personal stress/ conflicts. It is much easier to ensure personal health when we are supported by well-functioning, optimally healthy systems at other social levels. We need to clearly understand the impacts that these systems have upon our health and adaptive capabilities. And, of course, optimally functioning people desire and actively support the highest heath potentials and quality of life for friends, family, and colleagues.

Another strategy is that of prevention. What are we trying to prevent? Those poor personal health habits and health behaviors which lead to less than optimal functioning in the short-run and to ill health (disease) in the long-term. The goal of prevention is to take steps to combat or reduce risk factors before they create major problems sometime in the future. Let us now explore the use of terms that are traditionally applied to disease pre-vention in the area of health behavior prevention.

Primary behavior prevention means using early interventions to enable individuals or organizations to avoid behavioral problems that might be-come very damaging in the long run. It is based on the idea that the entire work population can benefit. The goal is to promote productive behavior and positive strengths rather than to react, heal or restore after positive functioning is no longer possible. Primary prevention has not generally been effectively utilized because it is quite difficult to accomplish. One of the objectives is to educate people to alter risky, unhealthy habits and in-effective behaviors. A stress reduction program is a good example of the difficulties encountered in primary change prevention because detrimental effects of stress may not be seen for many years. Stress responses are well-practiced, nearly immediate, and largely unconscious behaviors that may not be perceived by the individual as unhealthy. Another even more effective, yet difficult, approach is to teach people to avoid developing bad habits in the first place. For example, the "Just Say No to Drugs" program is aimed at elementary school children.

Secondary behavior prevention means that one responds to a situation that has created some problems which have not yet reached crisis dimensions, but it is too late for primary prevention. By catching them as early as possible, problems can be addressed before they develop into full-blown behavioral and health problems. The objective is to lessen the impact and extent of the problem. We see the importance of early identification (detection) and treatment (restoration) that reduces risk by emphasizing healthy lifestyles.

Tertiary behavior prevention means that the situation has already deteriorated substantially and the problems have become serious. The objective is to reduce the consequences of severe dysfunction after its occurrence. Here we are trying to alter well established, unhealthy behaviors. An example is a strict diet and exercise regimen designed to prevent recurrence after a heart attack. These interventions are the most difficult to make effective due to existing high risk factors and habitual behaviors that have already done their damage.

LIFESTYLES, BEHAVIORS, HABITS AND RISK
Lifestyle is the typical way we live today that combines our health and behavioral habits learned over a lifetime, regardless of our current age. In fact, our lifestyle will help to determine how long and how enjoyable our life will become in later years. The very idea of lifestyle indicates that we do have some choice and control over the quality of our lives.

Today, changes in the very foundation of our organizations and institutions present us with an enormous variety of workstyle choices and options. We might define workstyles as the work patterns, habits and behaviors that make up our work personalities. In our highly technological, mobile and information-rich society, we are quite ignorant of our potential and limits. In many ways, the opportunities for active, life-long learning are greater today than ever before.

Health behaviors are those positive actions that promote health and wellness. Reducing health risks requires a more systematic approach to behavior change. Health habits are behaviors that are well established and soon become habitual; they are performed automatically, and we are not consciously aware of them. For this reason, awareness through education and assessment is an important first step. We each develop habits because some behaviors have been reinforced by positive outcomes or rewards. These behaviors become habits if they are maintained through social or environmental reinforcement. The new behaviors then becomes independent of such rewards. Just turn on the TV and watch your family run to the kitchen for a high calorie snack of icf cream, soda and high sodium, high fat snacks. Such between meal snack habits are highly resistant to change. Hence, it is most important to establish proper eating habits early in life if we desire our children to practice healthy eating behaviors later.

What Influences Our Health Behavior and Habits
Each of us makes daily decisions that directly and indirectly influence our health. We know that such things as friends, media, church, family, clubs, school and business practices influence health behaviors and practices. Most of us display inconsistent patterns of health behaviors and habits. These health behaviors are influenced by perceived symptoms, social factors, (such as what our family and friends do), our feelings, and even access to medical care. Our specific lifestyle behaviors also impact health and work performance, but the impact is generally over the long-term. Over the short-term, the same poor health habits create vague feelings of being tired, run-down, and irritable. Such symptoms are then believed to be the inevitable. It is difficult to see that these bad health practices lead to serious diseases in later years, such as heart attacks, strokes or cancer. Illness and disease also has consequences for the organization, as resources are diverted from more strategic considerations.

Perception. Bad habits and behaviors determine the extent to which we feel well or optimally healthy and influence our sense of personal effectiveness. Many of these habits are influenced by how we perceive them. For example, if we feel that too many hangovers are keeping us from getting to work on time, we may stop drinking on certain nights of the week or drink earlier in the evening or with dinner to lessen the effects.

Conversely, a problem drinker might decide instead to take the edge off the hangover with an early morning drink and have a couple more at lunch time. Perception of negative and bothersome symptoms is often not enough motivation to change poor health habits. We need a more comprehensive approach.

Cultural Influences. Our culture and society also influences how we view health and why we develop and continue to practice bad habits. We live in a culture that implicitly sanctions productivity losses due to excessive eating, drinking, and smoking, while it promotes sedentary and stress-filled lifestyles. For example, our social/cultural norms encourage poor nutritional habits because we utilize a fast-food industry that is modeled after our fast-paced lifestyle. However, few ask how this industry has helped this lifestyle thrive and what we can now do about it?

Family Influences. Another set of social influences that impact our health habits are those norms, beliefs and values that we learned as children and adolescents. Our parents taught us certain health, eating, nutrition, exercise and leisure habits. We learned about such important family values as how much food was proper to leave on our plates, whether or not to take vitamins, or even to discusshealth issues. Today we find more families who take responsibility for educating and socializing their children about the importance of healthy lifestyle choices. In addition, our spouses and children can either support or sabotage our desire to change our unhealthy habits. The reasons are not always obvious, but may depend upon whether the new behavior creates a problem for our loved ones, such as changing family schedules for new exercise program, or a family member's new food preferences. This is why it is very important to involve all family members in health promotion activities.

Peer Influences. Friends and peers are social influences that help establish our health behaviors by supporting such risky behaviors as smoking, taking drugs, or using alcohol. Peers have a particularly strong influence upon both the smoking and drug taking behavior of adolescents. Peers and workmates can also have a very positive impact upon our ability to change. Here again, we observe the need to use the leverage afforded by support groups in workplace health promotion programs if we are to significantly. change unhealthy health behaviors

Emotions. Emotional influences also impact our health behaviors. People often drink, eat and smoke excessively when experiencing excessive amounts of stress. Remember, a certain amount of stress is essential for active and productive living andwhat we perceive as stress is also important. A positive strategy is to substitute exercise for excessive eating or drugs when under emotional stress. Stress itself can increase under conditions of loneliness and lack of social support, so we need to think about ways of building social support and caring networks and services for those without them Mangers also need to become more aware of these issues.

Control. Workers today are more educated and more aware than ever before of changing trends around them. They also indicate the desire to become involved, participate more actively and contribute more productively to their careers and organizations. Employees at all organizational levels need to feel in control of their work lives, to make meaningful and responsible choices which integrate personal needs with organizational goals. Feeling in control of their bodies and health become even more important to employees when their ability to influence their work situations is lacking. In such situations, feeling victimized can encourage status-quo thinking, bad health behaviors, and even increase resistance to positive changes, such as organizational health promotion programs. How can we improve our ability to become more aware and sensitive to the effects of change on others, the stresses around us, the consequences of flawed personal decision making, the often destructive way we define and use power and control strategies, and the impacts that our personal handling of transitions exert upon our employees and organizations? We must begin with each individual's awareness, skill, knowledge and responsibility levels.

Responsibility. Personal responsibility is an important aspect of any individual's ability to lead or manage effectively. The responsible person has placed the power and control issues in proper perspective, and never passes problems upstream or downstream without making suggestions for their solution. Taking responsibility for one's actions and behaviors is essential to the process of making healthy choices and decisions. In spite of all the other influences, the decision to live a healthy life style is a personal one that can only be made by individuals who desire to believe they are ultimately responsible for their health behaviors.

Self-Esteem. A healthy self-esteem is a deep feeling of worth and value that is based upon self-awareness, a positive self-image, and realistic self-acceptance. Self-image is built upon the subjective perception of our strengths and weaknesses, indicating how well we accept who we are--either through positive feelings of confidence--or negative feelings of deficiency, insecurity and lack of self-confidence. One indication of good self-esteem is acceptance of work as a life-long learning adventure, full of marvelous opportunities and surprises. Probably more than any one attitude, the ability to draw positive lessons from failure is the key difference between those who succeed and those who become "failures." Leaders and employees with good self-esteem seldom waste time comparing themselves; they already know they possess value and desire to give their time and energy to assisting and caring for others. Their standards of comparison derive from within their being and pertain to personally meaningful concerns, not meaningful externally imposed games.

Can we recognize a damaged and unhealthy self-esteem in the workplace? The *self-deprecating doormat types* are easy for most people to recognize due to their need to please everyone and their failure to be assertive. *Habitual conflict-prone employees* often cause problems because they displace their feelings of low self-worth through attacks upon other's ideas and projects. More subtle is the *overachiever-controller,* who fearful of failure insists on perfection. This perosn can not ask questions, will not admit errors, has a difficulty in participating, and can not delegate effectively. The important thing to remember is that each person's level of self-esteem is not determined by race, sex, religion, or socioeconomic standing, although it is correlated with these variables

Commitment to Effective Change. Self-worth comes from the power of our own minds, our thoughts, and our behaviors..A healthy sense of ones self requires good self-management skills which can be learned. Learning better self-management skills and more effective behaviors requires only three key commitments:

> **First,** we must become absolutely honest with ourselves, identifying our strengths and areas for improvement. Many fear what such a rigorous search will yield!

> **Second,** we must keep open to possibilities, perceiving change as a life-long adventure.

Third, we must become willing to build upon those abilities and strengths in order to reduce our limitations.

With self-honesty and a positive perspective for planning and skill building, we will more likely achieve meaningful development.

BEHAVIORAL CHANGE AS A PERSONAL STRATEGY

Deciding to change is a very personal process. Since humans have a natural desire to do meaningful things, whether at work or play, they are always busy planning how to change their work or personal life in more positive and productive directions. This does not mean that they also know how to accomplish this task or how to sustain motivation once they begin the process. When we decide to change our unproductive or unhealthy behaviors, we are also striving for more meaning, balance and consistency in our lives.

Some types of behavioral change are more helpful, effective and productive, while other types are dysfunctional, unproductive and ineffective. Productive change occurs because individuals know who they are and desire new information for growth. Change in behavior does not mean that we now are perfect, but instead requires us to learn how to design effective support systems for more long-term development of meanging. Healthy and effective employees know that meaningful behavioral change helps them to live more healthy and productive lives. People need to feel involved and want to participate in those changes that point toward a better way of life and work. Employees want to feel that changes that they bring about will facilitate their emerging personal goals. It is almost impossible to change and manage our personal lives without some assistance from the larger activity going on within our work organizations, and our lives outside the organization: in families, neighborhoods, communities, regions, and the world.

People should ask themselves two important questions before becoming involved in a behavioral change activity: First, are the purposes and goals that are promoted by this program ones that I can believe in and work toward? Second, is this a well-organized program that will be an effective use of my time and will lead to my success? To really answer these two questions for yourself, you need to know your own priorities, values, needs, interests, and wants. What is important to you and does this program appear to help you achieve important lifestyle and health goal?. In addition, you must clearly examine what you are currently doing. Ask yourself how do you spend your time? What are the things that might detractv you from accomplishing what you want for yourself from this behavioral change program?

HEALTH PROMOTION AND BEHAVIOR CHANGE
This section is concerned with helping individuals to change negative habits and behaviors, including those that impact their health and its costs to their organization and to society. We will explore behavioral change strategies adopted from research. First, in order to meet system-wide goals, the organization must sponsor programs that effectively encourage positive skill development and behavioral changes. Any change program must take into consideration how people learn to change negative behaviors and ineffective work patterns.

FACILITATING BEHAVIORAL CHANGE
Personal development and learning activities, including those focused upon health promotion, should emphasize five aspects of change:

1. **Assessment and Feedback**--engageing in formal testing or complete HRA, initiating health awareness through attending orientation sessions, taking stock of behavior patterns, identifying the negative ones, personalizing the relationship between risk factors of certain destructive life-style behaviors and the diseases that can result, and finally, commitingt to changing them.

2. **Goal Setting and Planning**--identifying new behaviors and action goals that when properly followed, will actually lead, one step at a time, to success.

3. **Motivation to Act and Sustain Change** --following methods and practicing techniques and skills that are known to actually change behavior.

4. **Evaluating, Feedback and Monitoring**-- monitoring progress and reinforcing positive successes; mentally reviewing skills and practices that brought you to this point.

5. **Maintenance and Support**-- using the support and encouragement of others in your work group or family to maintain commitment.

A SAMPLE PROGRAM ORIENTATION AND START-UP

As we have stated several times, the primary rationale for any health promotion program is to provide a process that will assist the employee to attain a healthier lifestyle. The goal of health promotion is more then being free of sickness now. The ultimate goal is too reduce those risky lifestyle behaviors that may lead to degenerative diseases later in life. Health promotion is a proactive process for providing workers the opportunity to explore the possibilities for achieving an optimally healthy and satisfying wellness lifestyle today.

Any promotion effort must begin with a bang! Health promotion is no exception. To start your program off with an energetic beginning, follow this five-phased process: 1) orientation; 2) testing or assessment; and 3) wellness feedback for goal setting and planning; 4) building motivation; and 5) monitoring and maintenance to sustain motivation.

Orientation. The orientation sessions are run in one hour segments that serve to inform and energize employees about the upcoming program. Topics covered include the following: Why wellness is a total approach to positive life enhancement and also fits the organization's goals. How behavior is affected by the workplace climate and culture. What are the relationships between lifestyle choices and the risk for developing disease later in life. Why awareness and self-assessment are important beginings for each person. How and why support systems are important. What the overall structure of the program includes such as the schedule of planned events and classes. Make sure to present this information with a human face and personalize it as much as possible--how poor health hurts you, your future job prospects, and your family.

The orientation session should be tailored to the personal needs of employees and culture of the organization. Tell them how and why wellness effects them and their family personally. Make orientation fun, as spontaneous as possible, and free of accusations that produce guilt and anxiety. This session should be highly interactive so that questions and involvement from the audience are part of the ongoing process, not just at the end of the session. The process should emphasize the team feeling created by the organization's interest in improving the quality of life for all workers and its desire to get as many employees involved as possible in making the program an organiza-tional success. Keep the emphasis on fun, growth and challenge, not rules and regulations. Distribute handouts at the end of the session. Do not be afraid to use an bit inspirational approach with an upbeat and positive tone.

It should be emphasized that the program is totally voluntary and all records kept confidential, with no chance of leaks.

Testing. The testing phase is given as soon after orientation phase as possible. Testing should be done in a non threatening and pleasant manner. You may also alternate the orientation and testing days to bring new people into the program. This phase provides an opportunity to ensure that all participants have an accurate assessment of their current health indicators and risks associated with their lifestyle practices. Testing may be done with a health risk appraisal, or if cost is a consideration, then the HRA can be done without the testing.

Feedback, Goal Setting, and Planning. The data gathered from testing serves as the focus for personal wellness feedback, counseling, and planning. This usually starts soon after the testing phase ends, when the results of the testing are tabulated and ready to be shared. During this phase, participants can perform a decision making exercise to help them to identify important lifestyle related risk factors that they may want to change. They may decide that they need additional personal counseling in fitness and nutrition, or group classes to help them to sustain their motivation. The data from either testing or the HRA provides important information that can provide a later baseline measure of the program's ongoing effectiveness.

The motivational modules for specific personal change (stress, nutrition, weight management) and healthy lifestyles begins after the counseling, goal setting, and planning. We will explore some issues in specific behavior change in the next sections.

Let us review the key features up to this point. The health promotion program is for your employees' and organization's benefit. The mission is to assist employees in achieving more optimally healthy lifestyles and to provide the environmental supports to accomplish this. We can, of course, list more diverse and specific goals for the program, such as increasing morale, reducing absenteeism or health care costs. We will accomplish these objectives by helping employees to improve their overall health, energy and life satisfaction. We will experience even greater success if we provide various learning and skill building opportunities at the workplace, and support the process through management education, environmental modifications, clear communication, cultural and policy supports.

A MODEL FOR A PERSONAL CHANGE AND /OR WORKSHOP

ASSESS

The first stage requires some form of assessment, based upon either health testing or self-scored instrument, like the HRA, information from a recent visit to the doctor, or a yearly physical examination. Individuals should also assess some of their lifestyle behaviors through a variety of instruments that are now available. Assessments show the interested employee where they currently are located with regard to healthy lifestyle behaviors, and thus allow them to set more realistic behavioral change goals. Assessments provide each worker with a picture or profile of their risky behaviors that must be changed in order to produce a heathier lifestyle and reduce the chances of dying prematurely. The emphasis should always be on those behavioral patterns over which the individual has some control.

Next, the individual must develop the interest and motivation to acquire new assessment skills and knowledge. This can then lead to attempts at change that produce more personally meaningful outcomes. (i.e., "I tried that technique and it seems to make a difference.") This process further personalizes the link between behavior and health as the individual begins to see that changes in one area of their life has positive impacts on other life dimensions.

Some individuals will begin at an early stage to feel more confident about defining personal health risks and modifiable behaviors: smoking, weight, diet, exercise, and stress) People will quickly learn to differentiate those unmodifiable factors over which they have little direct control, such as heredity or an unhealthy environment. Finally, some people will broaden their involvement, find support (friends, colleagues, family, boss), and begin to set goals and plan based upon a more clearer picture of their abilities and interests.

SET GOALS

The goals of health promotion programs that are best achieved by individuals reduce both their illness behaviors and risk behaviors. The key is to focus upon those lifestyle behaviors that the individual has some control over and, thus, some possibility of changing (for instance, smoking, weight reduction,or stress reduction). Personalizing the link between lifestyle and work behavior in order to facilitates desire to change. However, it must be clearly presented that negative health habits do not cause disease, but do confer a probable risk of developing disease in the future. Our specific goals are to help individuals to:

1. Recognize personal responsibility for assessing their behaviors.
2. Use reliable intervention methods.
3. Develop a plan to change negative behaviors (discussed further in chapter 5.
4. Practice the recommended new behaviors and encourage the organization to develop supports, policies and reward structures for these new behaviors.

Goals should be:

1. **Specific**--Goals need to zero in on exactly what it is you want by answering the questions: where, and how, and what.
2. **Time-limited**--Your goals must be given immediacy by setting some time limits for their resolution.
3. **Possible**--In their enthusiasm to accomplish a lot quickly, many people are tempted to set a goal like losing too much weight in too little time. Be realistic and remind yourself that remaining at normal weight without a constant struggle should be the long-term objective.

Sample Goals

Now, let us set some sample goals by answering the following questions:

1.   **WHERE do I want to go?** (My long term goal) EX. I comfortably maintain _____ pounds or 17 % body fat % by practicing good eating, exercise and and lifestyle habits. I intend to learn about wellness and live a wellness lifestyle and take all courses in our new wellness program.

Goal

_____

_____

2.   **HOW am I going to get there?** (My intermediate goal). EX. Having identified the habits important to my success (eating and exercise), I am practicing to make them com pletely automatic. I learned this through the four week course I took in nutrition.

Goal

---

3. **WHAT am I going to do first (next)?** (My immediate goal) EX. I am in control of my food intake and energy output now by monitoring the calories in all foods I eat!
Goal

PLAN

Planning takes into consideration needs, values, interests, and current risk factors that might influence employees' ability and willingness to change. If they do this, their choices regarding what and how to change will probably include an increased commitment to the behavior change process. The areas chosen for the health improvement or enhancement plan should also have the highest probability of success. This initial successes will also increase the chances of sustaining behavior change improvements over time. Lasting changes, thus become incorporated into workers' lifestyle behaviors. But behavior change requires more than motivation; good information about the best strategies for change are also needed! For example, there is no greater exercise in willpower than that shown by dieters who have cut their calories drastically. However, the evidence of research also suggests that people who constantly start and stop diets actually gain weight more readily. Thus, a "go it alone" approach may not be enough for some people. A self-help manual may help. However, all the information in the world will do some people no good if they do not possess the needed skills to make the right behavioral choices. Finally, perhaps they might join or utilize a support group. This choice might mean the difference for someone who needs the encouragment and support of others to succeed. Assessment, motivation, goal setting, skill building, planning, and support must work together if employees are to successfully reach their goals.

GETTING AND STAYING MOTIVATED

Of course, many activities can provide much relevant foundational knowledge to begin the process, but the choices and decisions to plan priorities and act effectively for oneself, one's career, and one's organization must eventually be a personal decision that is the result of becoming personally motivated to action. The secret to reaching one's goal is to build upon initial enthusiasm by providing the opportunity to succeed which helps to sustain enthusiasm and build motivation. The goals must be reasonable in order to successfully reach them. Any change takes time, but those people who expect to achieve more success than is reasonable within a given amount of time are rarely able to sustain their motivation long enough to reach their goals. They are really setting themselves up for failure.

The following tips can help sustain motivation. Actions speak louder than any planning or assessment up to this point. The process of behavior change for positive work and lifestyle habits begins with developing a new perspective through information. This information makes the prospects of behavioral change at least intriguing, interesting, or meaningful. Individuals must perceive the connection between behaviors and positive functioning (high level health or wellness), to be personally real, relevant and necessary.

MOTIVATION ASSESSMENTS
Positive motivation as it applies to the solution to a behavior/health problem can best be seen as a learned skill. Unlike the common perception of motivation as a force which acts on us from without, true self-motivation is developed from within through the application of specific, definable techniques. It begins with energy and comittment that you can accomplish your desired objectives, regardless of the odds. It ends with a feeling that skills to change have been learned and will now help support a new range of lifestyle behaviors.

The obstacles to change are numerous. Your friend's or spouse's desire for you to change, to get a raise or promotion or to lose weight is not alone enough to motivate you toward that end. You must recognize for yourself the need to change, to improve, and have a desire to do whatever is necessary to get the job done. The statements below are characteristic of a highly motivated person. **Check** the ones which apply to you.

[ ]   I frequently review the goals I have set for long-term behavioral change (exercising more, creating a new wellness program, improving weight control).

[ ]   I reward myself for small successes that keep me inching toward my goals. I know that the foundation for building anything lies in mastering the building blocks with enthusiasm, perseverance and a commitment to quality.

[ ] I frequently visualize myself in the future reaping the rewards for successfully achieving my goals.

[ ] I no longer have high peaks and deep valleys in my motivation. I can sustain a level of quiet confidence because I know where I am going and how I am going to get there.

[ ] I dwell on and affirm the things that I value and am no longer fearful or anxious that the things I do not desire or support will come to pass. I do not dwell upon negative thoughts. However, I am receptive to feedback and know that I can learn a great deal from my mistakes.

Take heart if you could not check all of these positive statements at this time! By listening, reading, and taking in a behavioral change health promotion workshop, you gradually change your negative lifestyle habits. We have already explained that this process does not call for quick-fix solutions. It is entirely possible that you were highly motivated when you started your last attempt at behavioral change (stopping your destructive arguments, improving your diet, starting to exercise, stopping smoking, no more procrastinating).

Check the statements below that accurately reflect your experience with trying to maintain motivation:

[ ] When I begin programs or regimens to change my behavior (like poor performance, being late to work, improving exercise patterns or diet), I hear the music of "The Rocky Theme," but this tune turns to "Taps" by dusk of the 10th day.

[ ] I have been known to reward myself for being "good" (writing that book I know I can write or staying on my diet)--by being "bad" (procrastinating or asking for one more order of fries).

[ ] The last time I successfully "made" a goal, I was playing basketball.

[ ] It is easy for me to think positivly--until it looks like things could possibly go wrong.

[ ] I can stay motivated until I stop and think about what it is I must accomplish. Then I do something dumb (lose my temper, forget to attend the seminar I signed up for, raid the refrigerator) and try to forget.

If the above statements apply to you, the first step is to introduce you to some simple techniques that will help you build and sustain positive self-motivation. For many people who are seeking to gain control over a behavioral, work or-health concern, the ability to build and sustain their motivation toward a worthwhile goal is the difference between a glowing success and a frustrating failure.

Below are some techniques that have proven to be successful in sustaining motivation.

Write Clear Goals. After you have determined what you want, the next step is to set some written goals that clearly state what you expect to achieve in the short, medium, and long term. Do not forget to review these goals daily (or many times a day if needed) in order to keep your goals in your mind.

Visualize Success. You next need to develop mental pictures of yourself achieving these goals and reaping tangible rewards. This includes the development of mental images of yourself that are compatible with a person who is successful. We will help you do this in two ways; through self-visualization and through a process known as affirmation.

Recognize Progress. You need to become a "doer" who is not concerned with perfection, who sees "failures" (there is really no such thing) as important learning experiences, the kind of person who realizes that there are many steps leading to the final destination. As long as you are making progress, whether measured in inches or miles, you are moving closer to your goals. This is important because motivation is sustained by seeing and feeling progress. For example, during the first 10 days to two weeks, dieters can easily see the results on their scales. Despite feeling deprived, they can usually succeed because their weight is consistently dropping. But what happens when they reach a weight-loss plateau? When the only way they measure progress fails, they become quickly demoralized.

Reward Small Successes. You need to plan how you will tangibly reward yourself when you accomplish the steps leading to your ultimate goal; give yourself credit for small, as well as big successes. Thinking about the obstacles to goals will also help you to proactively anticipate and develop strategies to handle them before you let failure defeat you. Obstacles can be anything that prevents the practice of new behaviors at work: feelings, lack of skills or information, lack of clear goals and plans or the negative work environment

WEIGHT MANAGEMENT: BACKGROUND INFORMATION

Millions of workers are involved in weight reduction programs each year. With the number of undesirable weight loss programs available and a general misconception by many about weight loss, the need for guidelines for proper weight programs is apparent. Based on the existing evidence about the effects of weight loss on health, physiological processes and body composition parameters, the *American College of Sports Medicine* has made the following recommendations:

1. Prolonged fasting and diet programs that severely restrict caloric intake are scientifically undesirable and can be medically dangerous.

2. Fasting and diet programs that severely restrict caloric intake result in the loss of large amounts of water, electrolytes, minerals, glycogen stores, and other fat-free tissue (including proteins within fat-free tissues), with minimal amount of fat loss.

3. Mild calorie restriction (500-750 k calories less than the usual daily intake per week) will result in a smaller loss of water, electrolytes, minerals, and other fat free tissue (muscle), and is less likely to cause malnutrition. This strategy takes a more long-term approach to permanent weight loss.

4. Dynamic exercise of large muscles helps to maintain fat-free tissue, including muscle mass and bone density, and results in loss of body weight. Weight loss resulting from an increase in energy expenditure is primarily in the form of fat weight. Thus, an increase in energy burned through exercise can allow you to reduce the number of calories on a weekly basis that you must lose strictly through caloric reductions.

5. A nutritionally sound diet of mild calorie restriction, coupled with an aerobic exercise program along with behavioral modification of existing eating habits is recommended for weight reduction. The rate of sustained weight loss should not exceed 1 kg. per week.

6. To maintain proper weight control and optimal body fat levels, a lifetime commitment to proper eating habits and regular physical activity is required.

Much more could be said concerning the start-up of a weight control component into a workplace health promotion program. Very few weight reduction programs adhere to the guidelines presented. Although it is easy to fault the programs brought to the workplace, there is some evidence to show that the success rate of workplace programs is better than communuty based programs. Fifteen percent of all dieters keep their weight off for one year after they complete a program. In fact, recent evidence relating to weight programs that incorporate workplace competitions shows excellent promise. Cultural norms usually strongly favor fad-type approaches that promise quick results.

Habits are not changed by adopting such approaches to weight management, and when dieters return to the real world of food, they simply return to their old style of eating and quickly regain the weight that they have struggled so hard to lose.

The *American College of Sports Medicine* believe that a desirable weight loss program is one that adheres to the following:

1. Provides a caloric intake not lower than 1200 k for normal adults in order to get a proper blend of foods to meet nutritional requirements

2. Includes foods acceptable to the dieter from the viewpoints of sociocultural background, usual habits, taste, cost, and ease in acquisition and preparation.

3. Provides a negative calorie balance resulting in gradual weight loss without metabolic derangements. Maximal weight loss should be 1 kg per week.

4. Includes the use of behavior modification techniques to identify and eliminate dieting habits that contribute to improper nutrition.

5. Includes an aerobic exercise program of at least three days per week, 20-30 minutes in duration, at a minimum intensity of 60% of maximum heart rate.

6. Provides that the new eating and physical activity habits should be continued for life in order to maintain the achieved lower body weight.

WEIGHT MANAGEMENT: A PROGRAM EXAMPLE

1. Assessment and Feedback--You have just engaged in some formal testing and completed an HRA instrument. Let us say that you have become more aware of how dangerous those destructive life-style behaviors relate to being overweight can become. You also have a cholesterol problem. You know that long-term damage and diseases can result from your life-style choices, and you are building a commitment to changing them, so you have finally decided to enroll in the health promotion weight management class.

2. Goal Setting and Planning--You are now ready to identify some new behaviors and action goals that when properly followed, will actually lead, one step at a time, to your weight loss success for the long-term. Remember, you need to set goals that are specific, measurable, and are achievable. The. key is to commit yourself in writing to somesimple, reasonable objectives, so that you get a better sense of direction.This process also increases your chances of starting and gaining some early successes. Actually saying what you want is an important first step in any behavior change program.

EXAMPLE:
I will increase my fiber consumption to 20 grams a day. Now you need a mini plan to accomplish this goal. Your plan should be as specific and concrete as possible. Some people need more detail and guidelines than others; so you might like to add intermediate steps. Check steps, time lines, and reinforcement schedules. Others may only need one step to reach this goal. I will list a few for you and suggest that you list your own steps to accomplish the goal: 1) Eat more fresh fruit each day; 2) substitute more healthy, oat, rice and regular bran cereals for breakfast; 3) substitute some grain and pasta meals for meat meals at least once a week.

3. Motivation to act and sustain those changes--You can now learn and practice specific techniques and skills that are known to actually change behavior. Let us say that you are anticipating several obstacles that have hindered your weight management efforts in the past. In order to build motivation and sustain it, you need to think about the benefits of identifying some of these obstacles and working to overcome them: 1)this will help you to overcome potential problems, build new habits and eventually reach your weight goals. Finally, you need to identify those skills that help you to identify and deal with obstacles:

4. Evaluating, feedback and monitoring--You must monitor your progress and reinforce positive successes by mentally reviewing the practice of these new skills. You can do this by writing down carefully the results of the attempt too practice this skill in your daily environment. For example, during a week try to monitor the signals that trigger an inappropriate urge to eat or overeat. Write a description on a chart that lists both the place (home, work. club, vacation) and situations, places, times of the day, thoughts, emotions and people present. When you discover problems, deal with them immediately and list the substitutes that you tried and the outcomes.

5. Maintenance and support--You must use the support and encouragement of others in your work group or family to maintain commitment to changing your weight. Studies have shown that individuals who are attempting to change behavior are more likely to succeed if they receive support from others. Gaining support is not always easy and we know that effective health promotion programs should help organize support groups for this purpose. Some of the ways that people in behavioral change classes have found to get support from others are the following: rewards from the organization, work group or family member; calls of support to inquire about progress or any help needed; joint attendance at classes and other programs; plan meals as a family; get the entire work unit in a weight loss competition; make a personal bet with friends or workmates; practice skills with others.

4

MANAGING STRESS

INTRODUCTION

Because stress is something that we cannot see or easily measure, and can only feel when we are sensitive to it, we are often unaware of its impact upon us. Individuals and organizations are experiencing many pressures and stresses brought about by numerous social, lifestyle, and technological changes. These changes pose both potential problems and opportunities for learning about how to better manage our personal health, lifestyle, and work relations. Change is a part of life. Without it life becomes monotonous. Challenge and the ability to assert some control over our destiny needs to become part of our motivation to excel.

Stress can be managed; you can make it work for you rather than against you. The mishandling of stress can create all sorts of health, family and work problems in the long-run. In addition, we need to establish more proactive life management skills and wellness strategies. This section will focus upon several aspects of stress, including: assessment (evaluating, assessing, taking stock of your life); interventions (learning methods, practices, techniques and new habits/skills); and how to implement change strategies for managing consequences. In order to successfully complete any of these aspects of personal stress management, we must begin with our understanding of the various conceptual dimensions of stress. The modern manager, HP consultant or professional must understand more than how to do something; they must understand why it is done, and when it is appropriate to do one thing rather than another.

WHAT IS STRESS?

Hans Seyle (1974,1976) defined stress as the body's nonspecific response to any demand placed upon it, whether pleasant or unpleasant. Seyle believed that since stress was the body's nonspecific response, then stress itself can not become responsible for negative outcomes. In fact, some people thrive on stress. The explanatory key for Seyle was the adapted limits of the human body. Each of us must become more aware of ourselves and not misjudge ourr capacities by pushing beyond our personal limits.

Girdano and Everly (1969:3) give a more scientific definition of stress as a *"fairly predictable arousal of the psycho-physiological (mind-body) systems which, if prolonged, can fatigue or damage the system to the point of of malfunction and disease."* Stress is really a combination of stressors or factors that elicit a stress response.

WHAT ARE THE THREE BASIC SOURCES OF STRESS?

The three general sources of stress (or stressors) are: 1) Your personal environment;you must make constant adjustments to such varied things as noise, weather conditions, time constraints, and threats to your well-being; 2) Your body;you experience stress when you are sick, when your nutrition is inadequate, when injuries occur, and when irregularities occur in sleep. Children and adolescents experience stress simply by growing; 3) Your thoughts/mind; you interpret everyday eventsin a negative way because you dwell on bad experiences. This is the one source over which you can exert the greatest control by making changes in the way you think. We will discuss specific ways you can work to eliminate these stressors later in this module.

THE NEED FOR STRESS

A minimal or reasonable amount of tension, stress and worry are actually necessary for a healthy life. In fact, it provide the challenge to get us focused and motivated. With the belief in our ability to master some life/work skills, we can expand our potential for success, even with temporary defeats.

Stress can help us to clarify and focus upon important life and work goals. So try not to avoid all stress: you can not anyway. In fact, good stress *(eustress)* is essential for motivating high performance. The key is to develop a productive perspective about your life priorities, the ratio and amount/type of positive and destructive stress in your life, and your stress response patterns (what is causing you the most stress). When we observe problems with our responses to stress, we must develop plans to change them. Bad or excessive stress (distress) results from stressors that constantly wear our bodies and minds down by overwhelming our positive problem solving strategies.

WHAT IS THE PHYSIOLOGICAL REACTION TO STRESS?

The release of adrenalin into our blood stream is known as the *General Adaptation Syndrome (GAS), or The Stress Response.* Our body is instinctively ready to "fight" or "flee". We do not need to spend much time reviewing the meaning of these ideas, but the physical impacts of either response on the body can be substantial. Although these physical responses vary in strength, length and impact, they follow a fairly simple pattern. The activator stressor(s) signals the hypothalamus in the midbrain (it is not clear whether the signal comes from the frontal cortext or elsewhere). This process activates the pituitary or master gland in the adrenal cortex and the autonamic nervous system (including adrenal glands at the top of the kidneys), and stimulates the production of increased amounts of catechamines, adrenaline and noradrenaline. These stress hormones can ravage even the healthiest body if exposure is prolonged.

STRESS AND THE MIND-BODY LINK

Stress is a product of our mind-body link. It often begins in the mind as an interpretation of the world. Our perceptions of opportunity and risk can lead us to a cycle of either positive or negative behavior. This cycle or system is only effectively changed by feedback. Everything we do has a learning lesson attached, if we are receptive to feedback. Failure is only hurtful if we draw too narrow boundaries and miss the learning opportunity. Without feedback we might suffer from boredom, lack of challenge and social isolation. When people need energy and the will to live, they often force themselves to try new jobs, projects, meet new people, or try some new challenges.Change creates pain for us, but also provides our greatest joy and adventures.

Life is truly a constant process of managing work and human relationships. Those who are good at deciding how to define and solve important problems, experience a type of euphoric stress from the challenge of making headway. Others, who have no skills for seeking good information, sharing resources, gaining supports, and joining team efforts, are overwhelmed by the sometimes lonely demands of daily life. The skills we learn and use determine our stress levels. Do we attack problems impulsively and end up feeling defeated and more insecure? Or do we take charge of our lives by learning the skills necessary to decide, organize, interpret and implement a successful, problem-solving process or plan for action?

To prevent feelings of failure and low self-esteem, we must learn good stress assessment and intervention skills and use them during times of uncertainty and frustration. Our inability to organize information into meaningful solution, creates low self-esteem, which then leads to poor performance and ineffective organizations. Excessive stress and increased tension can even result from the process of negative thinking itself. Tension levels increase as the images of failure become vivid in our mind. This is why it is important to visualize successful behaviors and understand that the process of negative cognitive appraisal is as detrimental to our well-being today as the tiger in the jungle was to the well-being our ancestors.

The mind that becomes fixated or preoccupied with sensations of uncertainty and fear of failure, soon creates stress overload, which prevents any open-minded exploration of alternatives. Left unattended, stress incubates, feeds on itself and actually attacks the body with long-term destructive consequences. In fact, scientists are today more comfortable with the term psychophysiological (impacts the body as well as the mind with disease) rather than psychosomatic, which denotes "its all in the mind." Tension and worry actually get locked into our body and mind, and detract from making good decisions. We must utilize our minds to productively visualize problem situations and their solutions. This mental imagery allows us to scan for relevant information and rehearse productive solutions to problems. We need to be free of excessive worry and fear of failure, in order to engage in trial-and-error learning, and use fantasy to positively project future success.

STRESS RESEARCH: SOCIAL READJUSTMENT RATING SCALE
Research by Holmes and Rahe *(Gutknecht, et. al., 1988)* led to the development of the Social Readjustment Rating Scale (SRRS), which measures the susceptibility to illnesses brought about by various possible lifestyle changes. The scale listed 43 specific life events occurring within the last twelve months, each carrying a unit weight (called Life Change Units or LCU'S. The most stressful event was death of a spouse (100 LCU'S), and the lowest was a minor violation of the law (11 LCU'S). This research shows how broad generic

life changes might impact our vulnerability to illness. However, it does not establish either a cause-effect relationship or the actual incidence of disease. In addition, this model emphasizes how major crises and changes in life events, rather than the cumulative tensions of minor daily hassles and problems upon our self-worth and ultimate stress levels. Without the proper perspective, problem solving and diagnostic skills, these bruises to our self-esteem can add up to the cause for our stress overload.

THE RESPONSES TO STRESS

Stressors vary in intensity or strength. They include a wide variety of physical, mental and social-psychological conditions such aslike too much noise or pollution, changing jobs or even taking on more responsibilities at work. Every change in our lives, whether good or bad, produces a stress response. When stressors begin to overload our adaptive abilities, we begin to exhibit symptoms of stress. People under stress often look, feel, and act agitated, nervous, fidgety and can not concentrate or think clearly. They look and feel depleted, passive, drained, depressed and may suffer from a lack of motivation. Some individuals may grind their teeth without realizing what they are doing. When under pressurepeople act hostile, angry and appear out of control. Most can sense that they feel different and something is out of control in their lives.

We each have a unique way of perceiving the world and responding to stress. Our tolerance and ability to control the negative effects of stress results from our ability to recognize stress signals. Without this self-awareness, we experience stress overload. We must become more aware and better respond to stressors before they create problems. We are able learn these skills by assessing, observing and practicing how to improve our response to stress signals. The hardest task for those trying to manage stress is to improve their stress identification skills. *Adams (1978:166-168)* has identified four major categories of stressors:

1. **The changes at work:** including job changes such as increased work hours, increased responsibilities, more travel, reorganizations, mergers, changes of work pace and activity level.

2. **The non-work related, major life changes:** including taking on an expensive mortgage, other family finances, increased drug use, pregnancy, sexual difficulties.

3. **The daily pressures on the job:** including limited feedback, poor communication with your boss, unclear job assignments or responsibilities, excessive work and many tight deadlines.

4. **The external environment:** like noise, air pollution, increased traffic and congestion, general concern over the economy, empathy with increased numbers of children who are victimized by unconcerned adults, etc.

There are five major types of reactions to stressors:

1. **Subjective:** anxiety and low self-esteem
2. **Behavioral:** accident proneness, excessive eating, and impulsive behavior.
3. **Cognitive:** the inability to concentrate, forgetfulness, and hypersensitivity to criticism.
4. **Physical:** high blood pressure, increased glucose levels, dizziness and ulcers.
5. **Organizational:** increased absenteeism, lower productivity, high turnover, and higher incidence of work related health, accident, or disability claims.

HOW DO "LITTLE HASSLES" LEAD TO BIG PROBLEMS?

For the vast majority of employees, the most immediate source of stress or "stressors" are the "little hassles" which disturb the working day. Most workers can more than adequately fulfill their job description. Competence is seldom the issue. Studies and self-reports from working people indicate that it is the minor hassles which constitute the major source of stress in the workplace, especially for office workers. Prior even to these office or work hassles, small troubles at home can carry over and create stress at work. Hassles which plague people every day may be more injurious to mental and physical health than major, traumatic life events.

Hassles
1. Concern about weight.
2. Health of a family member.
3. Rising prices.
4. Home maintenance.
5. Too many things to do.
6. Misplacing or losing things.
7. Yard work or outside home maintenance.
8 Investments, or taxes.
9. Crime.
10. Physical appearance.

None of the foregoing may be on your list, but chances are good the small hassles contribute to you current stress levels.

HOW IS STRESS RELATED TO JOB PERFORMANCE?

It is now largely established that improved job performance is linked to decreased stress up to a certain point, but that a point of diminishing returns is soon reached. Excess stress causes performance to deteriorate, whether the task is balancing a checkbook or determining a corporate fiscal policy. This upside-down U-shaped, curvilinear relationship between stress and performance is known as the "Yerkes-Dodson Law." At the center of the curve is the "performance zone" where manageable stress results in high efficiency and productivity. Too little stress at the bottom end of the curve, or too much stress at the top end, cause performance and efficiency to decrease.

Among the many implications of this simple law or principle is that each person has a unique "performance zone"even further varies from day to day. When individuals are within their optimum performance zone, stress results in feelings of energy, excitement, and stimulation, and decisions are readily made. When conditions of stress are nonexistent or overloaded, the stress indicators are quite similar, resulting in irritability, a sense of time pressure, diminished motivation, as well as poor judgment and accidents. Fortunately, it is possible for each person to become aware of these factors and develop his or her own unique manner of achieving and remaining within the performance zone.

WHICH OF THE FOLLOWING SITUATIONS CAUSE YOU DISCOMFORT AND MAKE YOU FEEL ANXIOUS OR "STRESSED"?

Several prominent researchers have identified the following stressors as most common to management personnel. Check the ones that may apply to you at this point in your career.

[ ] Work overload and excessive time demands and "rush" deadlines.
[ ] Erratic work schedules and take-home work.
[ ] Ambiguity regarding work tasks, territory, and role.
[ ] Constant change and daily variability.
[ ] Role conflict (e.g., with immediate supervisor).
[ ] Job instability and fear of unemployment.
[ ] Responsibility, especially for more people than one can manage effectively.
[ ] Negative competition (e.g., "cutthroat, "one-upmanship,"and "hidden aggression."
[ ] Excessive vigilance required in work assignments that promote divergent goals.
[ ] Ongoing contact with "stress carriers" (e.g., workaholics, passive-aggressive subordinates, anxious individuals.
[ ] Sexual harassment.
[ ] Accelerated recognition for achievement (e.g., Peter Principle).

[ ] Detrimental environmental conditions of lighting,ventilation, noise, or personal privacy.

It is possible you checked none of the above and yet still experience destructive stress. It is also possible that your body is reacting and producing a stress response to some of the above and you are not aware of it. With virtually all sources of stress, occupational sources included, the first step to better stress management is the simple recognition and identifying the source and the type of stressor.

WHAT ARE THE MOST COMMONLY REPORTED WORKPLACE PROBLEMS ASSOCIATED WITH DESTRUCTIVE STRESS?

Studies *(Gutknecht, et. al.,1988)* indicate that physical impairments resulting from stress in the workplace are as listed below in decreasing order of frequency:

1) Anxiety and/or Neurosis (25% of reported stress cases).
2) Depression (20%).
3) Stress-related, Psychosomatic Disorders (15%)--(Headaches, low back pain, hypertension, gastrointestinal tract).
4) Alcohol and Drug Abuse (15%).
5) Situational Adjustment Problems (10%)--(divorce, finances, death in the family).
6) Other Disorders (15%)--(severe mental and/or physical morbidity or mortality).

From the employer's viewpoint, these impairments show up in the statistics for absenteeism, reduced productivity, and disruption in the workplace.

WHAT ARE THREE POSITIVE STEPS I CAN TAKE TO MANAGE THE STRESS IN MY LIFE MORE EFFECTIVELY?

While stress is not the only thing that causes the physical problems, their occurrence would be diminished if we:

1) Were better aware of when the stress response was happening,
2) Could reduce the frequency of stress responses, and
3) Had constructive ways of handling them when they occur.

STRESS AWARENESS ASSIGNMENT

The purpose of this exercise is to help you pinpoint the times and events in your day that produce stress, identify the physical symptoms you experience after the stress reaction, and recognize your present way of handling them. Once you have identified these aspects of your stress you will be in a good position to take positive, corrective action. As you go through your day fill in the categories below. Additionally, for the next week.

STRESS MANAGEMENT MASTER LIST

DATE/TIME   STRESSOR   SYMPTOM FELT   YOUR REACTION

_____
_____
_____
_____

WHAT ARE THE THREE MOST COMMON DESTRUCTIVE STRESS REACTIONS IN THE WORKPLACE?

Individual response to occupational stress can fall into three basic styles: 1) workaholic behavior; 2) Type A behavior; and 3) burnout. Understanding the symptoms related to these is an important first preventive step.

1. Workaholic Behavior

Workaholic is a loosely-defined term which connotes an individual who is addicted to work itself, rather than the results of that work. Although the term is usually used in a negative sense, workaholics are not inherently detrimental to themselves or others. A relatively neutral definition has been proposed by Marilyn Machlowitz in **Workaholics: Living With Them, Working With Them** as *"people whose desire to work long and hard is intrinsic and whose work habits always exceed the prescriptions of the job and the expectations of those with whom or for whom they work."* "Machlowitz concluded from her research that, *"satisfaction with work and with life are more apt to be intertwined than mutually exclusive."* This finding is consistent with research in longevity in which job satisfaction has been determined to be a significant predictor of both health and longevity. At the negative extreme there are the impaired workaholics who are inflexibly addicted to work to the detriment of all other dimensions of their lives. Estimates are that approximately 5% of the working population are workaholics.

Workaholic Scale

Check the statements below with which you agree.

[ ]   1.My work is one of the most rewarding and fulfilling parts of my life.
[ ]   2. I would probably work just as much as I do now even if I had no need to work to support myself.

[]   3. One of my main goals in life is to find and do "work that is play."
[]   4. I use a daily priority list of "things to do" to help me make the best use of my time.
[]   5. Most of my friends would probably agree that I usually have a great deal of energy and I get much of this energy from my work.
[]   6. I frequently work on weekends and holidays.
[]   7. I am so involved in my work that it is difficult for me to take vacations.
[]   8. I frequently break dates and cancel appointments so that I can get more work done.
[]   9. My work is so much a part of my life that distinctions between "work time" and "time off" get blurred.
[] 10. My involvement in my work sometimes causes problems for my family and friends.

Extreme workaholic tendencies (eight or more) need to be balanced. Here are some suggestions for doing this: 1) focus on the aspects of your work that are most enjoyable and learn to delegate or minimize those that you dislike; 2) decide how much time you want to spend working and limit your work accordingly; 3) schedule open time into your work life, since breaks can actually enhance your performance when you return to work; 4) learn to say "no" to new demands on your time; 5) try to remain oriented toward the positive aspects of your work such as the freedom and opportunity to be of help to others; 6) place a value on time away from work; 7) remember to show your appreciation for your family and friends, since they often feel overlooked and unimportant in the busy blur of a workaholic's productive, but isolated lifestyle.

The good news for workaholics is that high productivity and performance are possible without the disintegration of your personal life, possible heart disease, or psychological burnout. But creating this situation requires insight and being willing to initiate small but vital changes in work performance and lifestyle.

2. Type A Behavior
Closely related to the workaholic orientation is **Type A, inflexible, time-pressured behavior**. This has become recognized as a risk factor in heart disease. The following feelings, attitudes, and behaviors are among those that have been used to describe the Type A individual: 1) easy to anger and has trouble controlling anger; 2) always in a hurry and feels driven to get things done; 3) is aggressive and has a strong need for power; 4) expects perfection from self and others; 5) impatient and is easily frustrated when

things don not work out as expected; and 6) unreasonably demanding. The profile below includes many of the characteristics typical of Type A behavior. In the space provided check the characteristics that describe you.

[ ]   1. I often think about work when I'm away from my job.
[ ]   2. I usually feel guilty when I'm relaxing.
[ ]   3. I often interrupt other people when they're speaking.
[ ]   4. I can't stand to watch other people doing tasks that I could do faster.
[ ]   5. I become irritated when traffic is moving slowly.
[ ]   6. I tend to eat my meals quickly.
[ ]   7. I always feel rushed.
[ ]   8. I enjoy challenging other people's statements and opinions.
[ ]   9. I believe that my success is due to my ability to work faster than other people.
[ ] 10. I often pretend to listen to other people even though I'm thinking of other things.

If you checked *more than four items*, there is a good chance that you have some *Type A tendencies*. This is not necessarily bad, but it is important for you to be aware of some of the consequences of the stress that can result from Type A behavior.

HOW DIFFICULT IS IT TO CHANGE IF I HAVE SOME TENDENCIES TOWARD TYPE A BEHAVIOR?

Many researchers believe that changing Type A behavior is easier than changing eating habits. Some simple strategies for change recommended by Carl Thoresen, a Stanford psychologist, include: 1) talking more slowly and less emphatically; 2) interrupting others less and focusing your full attention on what they have to say; 3) gesture less abruptly with your head and hands; 4) cut down on fidgeting and juggling, and 5) find humor in the situation.

Our society seems to reward typical Type A individuals by recognizing their accomplishments, admiring the speed at which they complete tasks, giving them promotions in the organization, electing them to public office. But what price are some of these people paying for their success? We do not ask you to change your personality simply because you may exhibit some of these characteristics. We would only ask that you take a close look at the ways in which your attitudes and behaviors contribute to stress, and then explore ways to modify some of these behaviors to lower your stress load.

3. Burnout

Among the characteristics of burnout are chronic fatigue, low energy, irritability, and a negative attitude toward one's self and one's job. In listening to individuals suffering from burnout, certain themes consistently emerge, such as "trapped or attacked," "need to get away or escape," feeling weighted down," "exhaustion or depletion," "sensation of emptiness and loneliness," "being blocked by obstacles or circumstances which are insurmountable," and finally, "giving up or drowning." At the workplace these personal feelings translate into difficulty concentrating on or making decisions, failure of short-term memory, and overall impatience, cynicism, irritability, and rigidity or resistance to new input and ideas. Burnout seems to have three phases: First, there is emotional exhaustion, a feeling of being drained, used up, and of having nothing more to give. Second, there is a cynicism, a callous, insensitive regard for people, a "don't knock yourself out for anyone" attitude. Finally, the burnout victim comes to believe that he or she has been unsuccessful and all job effort has been fruitless. Although burnout affects both men and women at every level of employment, it is not inevitable, and its treatment or prevention can be as simple as one executive's decision to "make sure that every day I sit down with a real person and talk about a real problem, instead of pushing paper around."

As with workaholic or Type A behavior, it is possible to asses burnout tendencies. Below is a self-administered scale which can indicate such tendencies. *Respond to this quiz by thinking back over the last six months of your life.* Read each question and then give yourself a score for each one, ranging from **"1" indicating "little or no change"** in the last six months in the item, **to "5" indicating a "good deal of change"** in the item. Allow yourself about 30 seconds for a response and add up the total number of points for a maximum of 75.

THE BURNOUT INVENTORY
Please **check** the items in the following that pertain to you.

[] 1. Do you tire more easily? Feel fatigued rather than energetic?
[] 2. Are people annoying you by telling you, "You don't look too good lately?"
[] 3. Are you working harder and harder and accomplishing less and less?
[] 4. Are you increasingly cynical and disenchanted?
[] 5. Are you often invaded by a sadness you can't explain?
[] 6. Are you forgetting appointments and deadlines?

[ ] **7.** Are you increasingly irritable, short tempered, and/or disappointed in the people around you?

[ ] **8.** Are you seeing close friends and family members less frequently?

[ ] **9.** Are you too busy to do even routine things like making phone calls,reading reports, or sending out Christmas cards?

[ ] **10.** Are you suffering from physical complaints (aches, pains, colds)?

[ ] **11.** Do you feel disoriented when the activity of the day comes to a halt?

[ ] **12.** Is joy elusive?

[ ] **13.** Are you unable to laugh at a joke about yourself?

[ ] **14.** Does sex seem like more trouble than it's worth?

[ ] **15.** Do you have very little to say to people?

Give yourself 5 points for each item checked. SCORE____. As with the previous workaholic scale and Type A checklist, **do not be alarmed if your score is high (51 to 75)**. These self-administered scales are not definitive by any means. Actually, the greatest value of such self-administered scales is to take the first step toward correcting burnout tendencies by recognizing them. Once the recognition occurs, it is then possible to consider alternative choices of action.

WHAT CHARACTERISTICS ARE PRESENT IN THOSE MANAGERS WHO SEEM RESISTANT TO STRESS?

Dr. Suzanne Kobasa of University of Chicago has defined certain qualities in stress resistant people. She studied 259 executives over a two year period. At the end of two years it was evident that the executives who remained healthy under stress had certain characteristics in common which Kobasa termed "hardiness." Those executives who remained healthy had an attitude toward life and their work which was high on commitment, challenge, and control, and they felt supported in that orientation. Kobasa found that the characteristics shared by the hardy executives were:

1. A sense of commitment to, rather than alienation from the various aspects of their lives;
2. A belief that they have control over their lives rather than feeling externally controlled, and
3. A search for novelty and challenge rather than familiarity and security.

TECHNIQUES TO HELP YOU MINIMIZE THE IMPACT OF THE STRESS RESPONSE.

Ultimately, your success in managing stress depends on your ability tolearn and consistently use one or more stress management techniques. Read each alternative below and decide which one(s) you will be able to initiate for each stressful situation you encounter.

Self-Talk. This refers to a technique in which you use your reasoning ability to stop a negative, destructive emotional response to a potential stressor. Use your reasoning skills to talk yourself through an emotional reaction by focusing upon the positives in the situation. This should be one of the first options you investigate when confronted by a situation that has previously controlled you. Most of the following alternatives are ways to deal with destructive stress once it has occurred.

Thought Stopping. This refers to the technique of stopping stressful thoughts as soon as you become aware of them. Follow these simple steps to implement this technique:

1. Identify your recurring negative thought patterns (e.g., "I hate feeling so stressed all the time." "I'm out of control of my stress.")
2. Write these thoughts down adding key words that describe a more positive or desirable alternative (e.g., "I'm gaining control of my stress and feeling better every day." "I'm consistently improving and I feel much better about myself.").
3. When you become aware that you are experiencing negative thoughts about yourself, yell "STOP." Do this mentally if you are in a crowd.
4. Then, plug in the new statement about yourself to develop a positive mental picture. Work to build this image for at least two minutes. Repeat as often as possible.

Deep Breathing Technique. This is the one alternative you can easily use every time you encounter stress and can be used in conjunction with every other technique. The major physiological benefit of this is an immediate reduction in your heart rate. Here is the simplest way to use this technique:

1. Take a deep breath, drawing oxygen deep into your lungs.
2. Hold this breath for 3 seconds.
3. Slowly exhale, forcing all the air out of your lungs.
4. Repeat this two additional times.
5. Wait one minute and repeat this exercise again.

Exercise. This can be used as a daily stress reduction technique and is highly effective when done aerobically for 20 minutes at approximately 70% of your maximum heart rate. (Consult your physician before beginning any new exercise regimen.)

Self-Visualization. This is another form of self-talk. Here are some self-talk images to practice that will help you see yourself as a calm and centered person who is not controlled by events and the people around you. Feel free to make up your own scripts.

1. I am calm. Nothing makes me upset. I am composed and in control at all times. Every day in every way I become more serene.
2. When I start to feel frustrated and angry, I simply identify the source and detach myself from it. I can easily separate myself from the source, and I choose not to identify with it personally.
3. I have a good sense of humor. I am funny. Laughing makes me feel good and less tense. When I'm frustrated I laugh a lot. I love to smile and laugh.
4. When my life becomes stressful, I remember my goals. I am patient. I know what I want and I ignore minor setbacks. I feel tranquil and positive when I focus on my goals.

The Relaxation Response. Dr. Herbert Benson has developed a highly effective technique that can reverse the bodily reactions that occur during the stress response. He reports that the same center of the brain that speeds up your biochemical processes when you are alarmed can be called upon to slow these processes down. This process is called the *Relaxation Response*. When this technique is practiced correctly and consistently it will cause your pupils, hearing, blood pressure, heartbeat, respiration, and circulation to return to normal.

Four components necessary to bring about this response are: 1) A quiet environment; 2) A mental device (a sound, word, or phrase repeated silently or aloud); 3) A passive attitude toward your environment; and 4) A comfortable position.

A relaxation technique:

1. Sit quietly in a comfortable position.
2. Close your eyes.
3. Deeply relax all your muscles, beginning at your feet and progressing up to your face.

Keep them relaxed.
4. Breathe through your nose. Become aware of your breathing. As you breathe out, say the word, "ONE" silently to yourself. For example, breathe IN...OUT, "ONE"; etc. Breathe easily and naturally.
5. Continue for 8 to 20 minutes. You may open your eyes to check the time, but do not use an alarm. When you finish, sit quietly for several minutes, at first with your eyes closed and later with eyes opened. Do not stand up for a few minutes.
6. Do not worry about whether you are successful in achieving a deep level of relaxation. Maintain a passive attitude and permit relaxation to occur at its own pace. When distracting thoughts occur, try to ignore them by not dwelling upon them and return to repeating "ONE.". With practice, the response will come with little effort. Practice the technique once or twice daily, but not within two hours after any meal, since the digestive process seems to interfere with the elicitation of the relaxation response.

Time Management. Almost all of us could benefit from better use of our productive time during the work day. If you consistently reach a point in the day when you feel frustrated and anxious because of your failure to accomplish what you felt was important, you are experiencing destructive stress. Awareness of the causes of poor time management is the first step to better use of this precious commodity.

Poor time management can cause stress, frustration, and lowered self-esteem which in turn can produce inactivity, stress, poor work performance, bad nutrition and overeating. Additionally, many people seeking a solution to their problems feel they must lower the priority they have placed on changing that particular behavior in order to be successful. The exact opposite is more often true. Failure to plan and to allow proper time for your goal attainment is a frequently occurring problem. You must learn to analyze your time utilization, set some time management goals, and discover new techniques for improving the way you use your time in order to change bad health habits.

Control of your time (and your life) does not mean becoming super-organized, super-busy, or preoccupied with every moment of your day as it slips by. Good time management allows you to be flexible and spontaneous. Too much organization is as ineffective as too little. Learning to manage your time effectively will not take away your individuality and freedom.

Nutrition. Good nutrition can help you insulate yourself from the physical symptoms of stress. Take the following test to help you determine some of the strong and weak points in this area of your life. **Check** the items that are true for you *(most)* of the time:

I eat or drink...

[ ] 1. Less than three eggs per week.
[ ] 2. No more than two cups of coffee or two cola beverages per day.
[ ] 3. Whole grain breads, and avoid white bread as much as possible.
[ ] 4. Four or more servings of grains each day (bread, pasta, rice, etc.).
[ ] 5. No more than 1 oz. of "hard" alcohol or two beers or glasses of wine per day.
[ ] 6. No more than one highly concentrated sugar item per day (candy, donut, cake, etc.).
[ ] 7. Two servings or more of low fat, high protein items per day (lean red meat, light chicken meat, dried peas or beans, or fish).
[ ] 8. At least two fresh fruits (or juice) per day.
[ ] 9. At least two servings of vegetables per day.
[ ] 10. No more than 1/2 teaspoon of added salt each day.

How to interpret your results:

If you checked two or less of the above items , your diet needs some immediate corrective action! If you scored between three and six your diet is marginal. If you scored seven or more your diet is probably fairly balanced. This test is one way you can gauge the progress you make in the area of nutrition. When you have implemented positive changes in your diet, take this test again.

SUMMARY OF THE STEPS TO SUCCESSFUL STRESS MANAGEMENT

Step#1   Become aware of your own stress and your stressors.

Step #2   Understand what stress is and the long-term negative effects it can cause.

Step #3   Become aware of some of your bodily responses to stress.

Step #4   Pinpoint the times and events in your day that produce stress.

Step#5 Implement proven techniques to help yourself eliminate as much stress as possible.

Step #6 Practice one or more positive stress reduction techniques to help yourself minimize the impact of destructive stress.

5

PLANNING FOR PROGRAM EFFECTIVENESS

INTRODUCTION

Planning the organizational health promotion effort begins with assessing the needs and interests of the employees at various levels.Assessment paints a comprehensive portrait of the current state of the organization's health, identifies some negative behaviors that might have impacted its health, and provides a view of the organization's resources. No planning effort will be effective unless these areas are clearly understood and documented. Any plans that are based on this information will be practical because they will accurately reflect the current needs and interests of all employees. Thus, it will then become possibler to mobilize all segments of the organization.

Key decision points will arise during the planning process. Among the questions crucial to moving forward with this effort are the following: Will upper management support the effort with their resources and commitments? Is the employee-employer relationship conducive to a successful effort? Can the needs expressed during planning be translated into clearly definable goals? Are the various groups in favor of a health promotion program for the right reasons? For example, the CEO wants a health promotion program that will improve productivity and reduce health care costs within a very short period of time. Is this realistic? Will there be access to the varied sources of information (needs, interest, health habits, frequency of disease and disability) and resources (budgets, personnel, space) that will be needed to complete a comprehensive assessment, plan, and start-up program. These are a few of the issues that needto be addressed before extensive planning begins.

PART I: CONDUCTING THE NEEDS ASSESSMENT
Three of the most important reasons to assess input from all management levels in a company are:

1. To help plan an overall effort that has a good chance of succeeding.
2. To enable all employees to feel a part of the program.
   System-wide ownership is important to success.
3. To sell yourself and the strengths of the program.

THE NEEDS ASSESSMENT QUESTIONNAIRE
To obtain the best possible picture of the organizational needs, interests, and issues, the health promotion planner or consultant should interview and survey employees at the following organizational levels, given the organization is large enough to have these positions:

1. The CEO (or management spokesperson for the CEO).
2. The Director of Benefits, the Human Resource Manager or Personnel Director.
3. One or more middle managers.
4. The Safety Officer or Risk Manager.
5. As many employees as possible.

The following examples of needs assessments address some of the issues that are important for effective program implementation. Each organization has special considerations, and these samples should be used only as a guide when preparing your own assessment questions and questionnaires. The best results are obtained when the questionnaire is supplemented with one-to-one interviews.

The Pre-Program Survey--This is a general survey that can serve many purposes. An outside consultant or a company coordinator may wish to use such a survey to determine the level of interest in health promotion within a company. Although the following instrument is not designed specifically for one-to-one interviewing, its concise format makes it an ideal interview guide to use with a busy, time-conscious employees.

THE PRE-PROGRAM SURVEY

Workplace Demographics   **Replies**
1. What are the number of hourly workers?   _____
2. What are the number of salaried workers?   _____
3. What are the total number of employees?   _____
4. What percent of the workforce is female?   _____
   Male?   _____
5. What is the percent of part-time workers?   _____
6. What are the workforce age breakdowns?   _____
                                                                _____
                                                                _____
                                                                _____
7. What percent of employees work shifts?   _____
8. What percent of workforce speaks Spanish?   _____
   Other?_____   _____
9. What percent of your workforce is represented by unions?   _____

Health Benefits Information
1. Have your premiums been increasing annually for health   _____
   and other related policies? If so, how much?   _____
2. What are the three major reasons employees sought health   1._____
   care in the past year, in approximate descending order by 2._____
   cost and by frequency?   3._____
3. Is your company self-insured for any of its health benefits _____
   (does company internally hold and disburse benefits or internally hold monies on behalf of its employees' health costs)?
4. Please identify the total number of Worker's Compensation claims for the last five years.
   Total cost of those claims. What level of increase have you had for these years?

   _____
   _____
   _____

5. What were the major reasons employees filed Worker's Compensation claims by both
   frequency and cost?

   _____
   _____
   _____

6. Briefly list the changes your company has made in the health benefits package in the past three years.

_____
_____
_____

Absenteeism and Turnover
1. What is the company's definition of absenteeism?

_____
_____
_____

2. Based on this definition, indicate the approximate percentage of absenteeism for the total workforce for the last three years.   _____

3. Is there a system for monitoring employee absenteeism?   _____

4. What is the company's definition of employee turnover?

_____
_____
_____

5. Based on that definition, what was the employee turnover rate for the last two years?

_____

6. Is there a system for monitoring employee turnover?   _____

_____
_____
_____

7. What are the most frequent reasons for employees leaving your company?

_____
_____
_____

Occupational Health and Safety
1. Does the company have a health and safety program?   _____

2. If yes, please describe briefly the main components of the program (written health and safety policy, safety committee, safety classes, etc.)

_____
_____
_____

3. What are the major physical work processes involved in the company's operations (welding, lifting, desk work)?

_____

_____

_____

4. What are the potential health and safety concerns that have been identified in your business operations, and approximately how many employees would you estimate might be exposed to those substances and/or processes (noise, heat, chemical, dust, radiation, and crowding)?

_____

_____

_____

5. What are the most frequent types of accidents in the past year (cuts, lacerations, back injuries, etc.)?

_____

6. How many accidents were reported last year (per 100 employees per year)?

_____

7. What kinds and how many health promotion activities has your company offered in the past?

_____

_____

_____

Policies and Behaviors Concerning Tobacco Smoking

1. Describe any current restrictions on smoking in your workplace.

_____

_____

_____

2. What is your best estimate of the percentage of employees who smoke?

_____

3. Describe litigation and/or Worker's Compensation claims that have resulted from smoking at your workplace.

_____

_____

_____

Reasons for Health Promotion

1. On a scale of 1 to 10, how would you rate the interest of top management in health promotion?

      1   2   3   4   5   6   7   8   9   10

2. On a scale of 1 to 10, how would you rate the support for health promotion among top management?

      1   2   3   4   5   6   7   8   9   10

3. On a scale of 1 to 10, how would you rate the support for health promotion among mid level and supervisoraltmanagement?

      1   2   3   4   5   6   7   8   9   10

4. Prioritize from the reasons listed below, why your company is considering offering a health promotion program.
   - A. Health care cost savings   ____
   - B. Increased productivity   ____
   - C. Human resource management   ____
   - D. Compliance with health and safety regulations   ____
   - E. Community public relations and organizational image   ____
   - F. Other:_____   ____

5 What type of activities in a health promotion program do you believe should be implemented?

_____
_____
_____

6. What short-term benefits do you expect to see for your company in a health promotion program? Long-term Benefits?

_____
_____
_____

Thank you for your time!

The CEO or Owner/Operator Survey. The following assessment will help determine the extent of upper management interest in and support for the health promotion effort. Additionally, it will provide perhaps the most important feedback for establishing clearly-stated organizational goals for the health promotion effort. Some questions might be better answered by others in the organization like the human resource manager, but you still will want to ask them of the CEO.

CHIEF EXECUTIVE OFFICER QUESTIONNAIRE

1. Briefly describe your company's past experience, if any, with a health promotion program, or with the idea of starting a health promotion program.

   _____

   _____

   _____

2. On a scale from 1 to 10, how would you rate the current level of interest in a health promotion program? Among:
   A. Management?   ____
   B. Employees?   ____
   C. Union representatives (if applicable)?   ____

3. What do you perceive to be the role of management in a health promotion program?

   _____

   _____

   _____

   _____

4. Assume that your company wants to implement or strengthen a health promotion program. Would your organization have to contend with any of the following barriers, and if so, how strong is it? (1 indicates "no barrier" and 5 indicates a "strong barrier")

   A. Few people at this company see the need for health promotion.   1 2 3 4 5

   B. Lack of employee/union interest.   1 2 3 4 5

   C. Lack of widespread management support.   1 2 3 4 5

   D. Doubt about cost effectiveness of a health promotion program.   1 2 3 4 5

   E. Not enough in-house expertise to implement a health promotion program.   1 2 3 4 5

   F. Insufficient funds to get a program started and keep it going.   1 2 3 4 5

   G. Firm's reluctance to become involved in activities that may be perceived as the individual's concern.   1 2 3 4 5

H. Are there any other potential barriers that will have to be overcome in order to implement a successful health promotion program?

_____

_____

5. What are the main potential benefits, for employees and for the company, from participation in a health promotion program?

_____

_____

_____

_____

_____

6. Please list the major reasons your company is considering a health promotion program?

_____

_____

_____

7. Based upon what you know about employee health problems and needs, what should be the first program component started?

_____

_____

_____

8. What program component do you think would be most cost effective?

_____

9. Assuming that the company started a health promotion program:

A. What department and who in that department would be responsible for managing the program?

_____

_____

B. How would employee/union involvement be handled?

_____

_____

_____

_____

_____

C. How would the program be coordinated with other related programs (safety, cost-containment)?

_____

_____

D. What would be the impact of consultants for the program?

_____

10. Health promotion programs have many possible implications. Please comment briefly on the following issues.

   A. Programs offered on company time.

_____

   B. Flexible work hours to accommodate program participation.

_____

   C. Record keeping systems for program evaluation and cost-effectiveness.

_____

   D. Budget allocations to cover program costs.

_____

   E. Personnel assignments to manage program.

_____

   F. Time for employee participation in planning and administration.

_____

G. Top level endorsement of program.

_____
_____
_____

H   Incentive and reward programs.

_____
_____
_____

11. At the present time, what factors most favor the successful implementation of a health promotion program? What factors would hinder the program's implementation? How can these adverse effects be minimized?

_____
_____
_____

12. Are there any additional comments you would like to make that have not been covered?

_____
_____
_____

Thank you for your time!

The Benefits Manager Survey--The primary purpose of this assessment is to determine the health cost management issues relevant to the health promotion effort. A few of these concerns are the following.

THE DIRECTOR OF BENEFITS SURVEY

1. Would you describe the health insurance premium history for the last five years?

_____
_____
_____
_____
_____
_____

2. What is the premium history for other health-related insurance for the last few years?

_____
_____
_____
_____

3. What is the percent of annual increase in health insurance premiums?

_____

4. What kinds of changes have occurred in the benefits package over the last few years, particularly health-related changes?

_____
_____
_____
_____
_____

5. Do you currently subscribe to an HMO or PPO?   _____

6. What cost-containment measures have you employed over the last few years?

_____
_____
_____
_____
_____
_____
_____
_____

7. How many sick days do your employees receive per year?   _____

8. What health cost related area(s) do you feel might be helped by promoting health in the workplace?

_____
_____
_____
_____
_____
_____
_____

Thank you for your time!

Human Resource Manager Survey--This person is usually, but not always, a strong ally of the health promotion effort. The internal manager/ coordinator of the HP program is likely to be a member of this department. Questions relating to absenteeism, turnover, and personnel policy are included in this survey.

HUMAN RESOURCE MANAGER QUESTIONNAIRE

1. How does your company define "turnover"?

    _____

    _____

    _____

    _____

    _____

    _____

2. Based on this definition, what is considered an acceptable rate of turnover in your type of business? _____

3. Does your company calculate these rates on a regular basis?   Yes   No   If answer is "yes," then could you answer the following:

    A. How frequently do you make this calculation?

        _____

    B. How detailed is the level of the breakdown of information?

        _____

        _____

    C. Is information broken down by sex, position, race?   Yes   No   If answer is "No", then could you readily calculate these rates if necessary? _____

4. How would you characterize your company's turnover rates?

    A. [ ] High   [ ] Low   [ ] Average

    B. [ ] Rising   [ ] Falling   [ ] Stable

5. What are the main contributing factors turnover in your company?

    _____

    _____

    _____

    _____

6. How does your company define "absenteeism"?

    _____

    _____

    _____

    _____

7. Based on this definition, what is considered an acceptable rate of absenteeism in your type of business?   _____

    A. What is your most recent estimate of your absenteeism rate?   _____

    B. Can this rate be broken down according to different employee groups, e.g., salaried, hourly, worksite, etc.? If so, which groups?

    _____

    _____

8. How often is the rate of absenteeism monitored?

    _____

    _____

9. Can you have estimate of the percentage of absenteeism due to disability and sickness?

    _____

    _____

10. How would you characterize your company's absenteeism rates??

    A. [ ] High   [ ] Low   [ ] Average

    B. [ ] Rising   [ ] Falling   [ ] Stable

11. Assume that your company decides to implement or strengthen a health promotion program. Would your organization have to contend with any of the following barriers, and if so, how would you characterize the force of the barrier? (1 indicates "no barrier" and 5 indicates "a major barrier."

    A. Few people at this company see the need for a health promotion program.   1 2 3 4 5

    B. Lack of employee or union interest.   1 2 3 4 5

    C. Lack of widespread management support.   1 2 3 4 5

    D. Doubt about cost effectiveness of a health promotion program.   1 2 3 4 5

    E. Not enough in-house expertise to implement a program.   1 2 3 4 5

    F. Insufficient funds to get a program started and keep it going.   1 2 3 4 5

    G. Firm's reluctance to become involved in activities that may be perceived as of the individual's concern.   1 2 3 4 5

12. Which of the following programs are offered by your company, and how useful do you feel these programs have been? (1 is "not very useful" and 5 is "very useful."

    A. Office Safety.   1 2 3 4 5
    B. Cardiopulmonary Resuscitation.   1 2 3 4 5
    C. First Aid.   1 2 3 4 5
    D. Low back Pain Prevention.   1 2 3 4 5
    E. Other:_____   1 2 3 4 5

13. Please describe the medical, nursing, or health staff available to your company, either by direct hire or other arrangement, that meets your company's needs regarding occupational health, general health, and/or health promotion services.

    _____
    _____
    _____
    _____
    _____

14. How do you assess the quality of these services?

    _____
    _____
    _____
    _____

15 If you could make changes in the capacity and/or characteristics of these services, what would you do?

    _____
    _____
    _____
    _____

16. What are the major potential benefits for employees and for the company, from participation in a health promotion program?

    Short term? (next year) Long term? (next 5 years)

    _____
    _____
    _____
    _____

17. Below are listed five reasons why companies typically desire to provide health promotion programs for their employees. Rank them in the order of their importance to you. Place a zero (0) by any that you feel do not apply to your company.

To increase morale	_____
To build human resources	_____
To improve productivity	_____
To show that you care	_____
To help contain costs	_____
Other: _____	_____

18. Based on what you know about employee health problems and needs, what should be the first program component started?

_____

19 What program component do you think would be most cost effective?

_____

20. At the present time, what factors most favor the successful implementation of a health promotion program?

_____
_____
_____

21. Would you like to add any additional comments about the prospects of a new or strengthened health promotion program?

_____
_____
_____
_____

Thank you for your input and your time!

The General Management Survey. If support from management and supervisory personnel is not obtained, your wellness program will likely fail. Frequently, the supervisors are in the best position to understand how the company is functioning and what the employees will and will not like. You should pay careful attention to their input.

This assessment can be conducted in a managerial group meeting, along with a HP consultant acting as a facilitator and asking the relevant questions. The group's replies might be recorded on a flip chart or white board. The managers can also be asked to respond to written questions.

THE GENERAL MANAGEMENT SURVEY

1. What kinds of obstacles to health promotion implementation might be expected from the line workers?

_____
_____
_____
_____

2. What kinds of programs do you feel they will want?

_____
_____
_____
_____

3. Do you personally think that promoting health is a good thing for this company to do? Why or why not?

_____
_____
_____
_____
_____

4. What potential problems will be presented by having your workers attend meetings during the workday?

_____
_____
_____
_____
_____
_____

5. What percent of your workers do you believe may have a problem with alcohol abuse? Other drugs?

_____
_____

Thank you for your input and your time!

The Employee Health and Interest Survey--Not only is it vital that you know what the employees think and feel about health promotion, you need to involve them so they can feel that they "own" the program, and that programs will address their personal health concerns and interests. While members of the planning committee can conduct one-to-one interviews, a questionnaire can be provided to all employees, yielding a larger number of respondents.

EMPLOYEE HEALTH SURVEY

I.   **Please fill in the following information about yourself:**

   1.   Personal data:
       A.   Height:_____Ft., _____ Inches tall.
       B.   Weight:_____Pounds.

   2.   Do you smoke?
       A.   _____ **No.**
       B.   _____ **Yes,** I smoke _____cigarettes on a normal day.
       C.   _____**Yes,** I smoke _____full pipes on a normal day.
       D.   _____ **Yes,** I smoke _____cigars on a normal day.

   3.   Have you had you blood pressure checked recently?   _____ Yes_____ No.

       A.   If "yes," what was your blood pressure reading?   _____/_____.

       B.   Have you ever been told by a nurse or doctor that you have high blood pres-sure or hypertension?   _____Yes_____No.

       C.   Have you ever taken medicine for high blood pressure? _____Yes_____No.

       D.   Have you ever been told by a nurse or doctor that your serum cholesterol level is too high?   _____Yes_____No.

   4.   Have you missed time from work during the last two years because of back pain?
                                                         _____Yes_____No
        If "Yes," How many work days?   _____days?

   5.   How many hours of exercise do you get each week?   _____ **Hours.**

   6.   How many times have you seen the dentist in the past year?_____ **Times.**

II.   **Please answer the following questions either true (T) or false (F).**
       1.   ___I plan to make changes in my health practices soon.
       2.   ___I feel I have too much stress in my life.
       3.   ___My job causes me to feel very stressed.
       4.   ___My behavior affects my health.
       5.   ___I always wear a seat belt when I ride in a car.
       6.   ___I drink two or more drinks of alcohol in a normal day.

7. ___ I am concerned that my work environment is not as safe/healthy as it should be.
8. ___ I have been told I have a drug or drinking problem.
9. ___ My health affects my ability to do my job right.
10. ___ My company should be concerned with my health.

III. **I would like to learn more about the following topics** (Check as many as you wish.)
1. ___ Weight control.
2. ___ How to stop smoking.
3. ___ Better use of my company benefit package.
4. ___ How to control my blood pressure.
5. ___ Cholesterol control.
6. ___ Improving my ability to manage stress.
7. ___ Exercising safely and effectively.
8. ___ Better nutrition.
9. ___ How to prevent back problems.
10. ___ Cancer prevention and detection.
11. ___ How to improve my time management skills.
12. ___ How to improve my communication skills.
13. ___ Conflict management.
14. ___ Other _____

IV **I would be interested in participating in the following activities here at work.**
(Check all that apply.)
1. ___ Workshops or classes on the topics checked on the preceding list.
2. ___ Films, videos, and lunchtime talks on the topics checked on the preceding list.
3. ___ An employee committee to help organize health-related activities.
4. ___ Special events, such as a picnic, health fair, or family fun run.
5. ___ Having accurate information available to me about health topics.
6. ___ Having my family join me in health-related activities here at work.

V. **Is there anything that we need to know about you or about your fellow workers that would help us to better plan to meet your needs?**

_____

_____

VI. **Do you have ideas or suggestions we should consider in our planning? If so, please explain your ideas in the space below.**

_____

_____

Thank you for your time and input!

THE SUMMARY REPORT

The Summary Report is a written from a compilation and integration of all data gathered from all the various assessments. It provides a composite picture of a given company's feasibility and readiness to implement a comprehensive health promotion program. The information gathered is frequently used to write a proposal. If you are writing a comprehensive summary report, information obtained throughout the assessment process can be categorized under various headings with each topic analyzed in detail. The report should be informative and succinct, since most decision makers value brevity and clarity. The following is a list of Summary Report categories with questions and examples of data that should be included.

THE SUMMARY REPORT

1. **Introduction:**
   - Date
   - Location
   - Names of persons involved in the assessment.

2. **Company Characteristics:**
   - Type of company?
   - How long in existence?
   - Number of locations?
   - Employees: How many? Type of work? Hours? Number of shifts?
   - Type of work environment: High tech? Industrial? Office. Management?
   - Employee relationships, communication between them?
   - Absenteeism and turnover rates? Possible reasons for high or low rates?
   - Unique personnel policies: Flextime, Welldays, Vacations?

3. **Benefit carriers**
   - Who are the insurance carriers? HMO options?
   - How are benefits determined? Employee contribution or employer pays all?
   - Increases in annual premiums over time? Possible reasons for the increases?
   - Number of claims filed? Frequency per family?
   - Average cost per claim? Categories of claims?

4. **Worker's Compensation and Accident/injuries**
   - Self-insured?
   - Is there a tracking system to identify nature of worker injuries?
   - How many claims? How are they monitored?
   - How many accident/injuries? How are they monitored?
   - What are the causes? What is the frequency? Highest to lowest incidence?

5. **Occupational Health and Safety**
   A. Health and Safety Program Policy Assessment:
      1. Employee education and training.
      2. Safety orientation.
      3. Self-inspection.
      4. Accident and illness investigation.
      5. Safety committee (and/or foreman/crew meetings).
      6. Record keeping.

   B. Health and Safety Walkthrough Assessment: Physical layout: breakdown of departments and number of employees in each potential/possible concerns, to include, but be not limited to:
      1. Lighting.
      2. Noise level.
      3. Crowding.
      4. Work station conditions: chairs, desks, ventilation, housekeeping practices.
      5. Need, availability, use of protective equipment.
      6. Inhalation of hazardous substances.
      7. Warning signs.
      8. Labels on containers.
      9. Other.

6. **Prior Experience with Health Promotion**
   What was done? Health fairs, screening, classes, seminars? Current committees? Management support? Response to past experience? Reasons for success or failure?

7. **Health Promotion Program Strengths**
   Factors which may favor implementation are:
   A. Corporate culture conducive to improving employee health and enhancing employee development.
   B. Positive prior experience.
   C. Management/employee support.
   D. Long-term perspective toward human resources management.
   E. Specific area/location and standard hours.
   F. Well-developed internal communications system.

8. **Health Promotion Potential Constraints**
   A. Lack of space/facilities.
   B. Uncertainty about funds.
   C. Insufficient data on medical claims utilization picture.
   D. Widely disparate attitudes among staff.

The Summary Report can be presented to the key decision makers in verbal, written, and visual forms so they can decide whether or not the company will implement a comprehensive health promotion program. Be sure you know what action you want from management and persent that request clearly. Is it budget approval for the program, or do oyu need approval to continue or start implmention by a certain date? Anticipate any questions top management might ask and be prepared to answer them effectively.If the decision is made to delay or not to implement a health promotion program, the Summary Report remains of critical importance to the company. For many companies this will be the first time data has been gathered and analyzed to provide a complete picture of employee health status and company health care spending. If the company decides to establish or expand a health promotion program, the information provided through this assessment process will be valuable in planning, developing and promoting the program activities. The company is now in an appropriate position to make informed, knowledgeable decisions about building a health promotion program that is more likely to succeed.

TAKE THE NEW WORK ETHIC INTO ACCOUNT
Any planning effort must take into consideration the employees' values and perceptions. Some researchers *(Gutknecht, 1988)* have identified certain changes in values they believe are indicative of a new work ethicincluding:

1. Dissatisfaction with the nature of work.
2. A need for more participation in the workplace decision-making process.
3. Dissatisfaction with authority.
4. An increase in the pursuit and importance of leisure time.
5. Development and reinforcement of personal identity outside the workplace.
6. A need for self-esteem, support, creativity, and affiliation from work rather than exclusively from a need for security, power, and status.
7. A need for control, autonomy, and freedom over work tasks.
8. Feelings of stress, uncertainty, insecurity, and anxiety due to rapid changes in ev eryday life.
9. A need for work to have personal meaning and purpose.
10. An increasing role for women in leadership.
11. A need for equitable balance between productivity and human satisfaction.

Health promotion programmers must learn to track and understand these changes and values in because of their obvious impact on both a changing work force and health enhancement projects.

THE HUMAN RESOURCES APPROACH TO PROGRAM PLANNING

Many workplace health promotion programs fail before they begin, dying in the planning stage. It is important to examine why programs sometimes fail if we are to understand their full potential for promoting health in the workplace. As mentioned in chapter one, health promotion should be conceptualized as part of a comprehensive approach to the investment and development of the organization's human resources.

Planning Objectives.

The human resource investment approach is needed in the field of health promotion because of the complexity of the human, social, organizational, and program challenges facing those involved. The effectiveness of health promotion programs can be increased by meeting the following effective people investment and management strategies:

1. Identify work and health problems areas.
2. Pinpoint existing problems in the organization that might effect program success.
3. Increase cost-effectiveness of the program by looking at the "big picture."
4. Provide data useful in program planning and goal setting.
5. Increase program impact by understanding the organization.
6. Encourage participation and support throughout the organization.
7. Increase long term benefits and provide follow-up data on emerging problems, trends, and challenges.
8. Create data helpful for further planning, manpower, and human resource concerns of the organization.
9. Create a business plan for the health promotion program.

A comprehensive approach to workplace health promotion planning involves people factors, program factors, and organizational factors. The following is a checklist of these three important factor items to be sure that essentials to success are included.

I. **People Factors**
    ___ 1. Employees' involvement in planning.
    ___ 2. Clear statement of incentives.
    ___ 3. Affect on participants' families.
    ___ 4. Avoid use of negative motivators (using blame and guilt to motivate change).
    ___ 5. Is program relevant to needs of workers?
    ___ 6. Assurance of confidentiality and volunteerism.
    ___ 7. Program's affect on the corporate culture.
    ___ 8. Motivation for long-term changes.

II. Program Factors

_____ 1. Location and length of program.

_____ 2. Follow-up to program.

_____ 3. Evaluation of design.

_____ 4. Realistic goals for program.

_____ 5. Do goals of program coincide with participant's goals?

_____ 6. Has needs assessment been considered in planning?

_____ 7. Do program goals identify risk factors?

_____ 8. Are facilitators adequately trained?

_____ 9. Communication of program goals?

_____10. Does the HP program have a business plan and budget?

III. Organizational Factors

_____ 1. Has program matched employee needs with organization goals?

_____ 2. Has a proper timetable been set up? Do employees have time to participate?

_____ 3. On-site or off-site participation?

_____ 4. To what degree is program addressing six wellness dimensions?

_____ 5. Will program be specifically tailored to employee needs? Is there a pilot program?

_____ 6. Have resistance factors been identified?

_____ 7. Have potential ethical issues (i.e., drug policy & smokefree work-place) been taken into account?

_____ 8. Is there a commitment by company to support long-term positive changes?

_____ 9. Are there unresolved labor/management issues?

_____10. Can health promotion be connected with other employee assistance programs?

_____11. Who will pay for the program and does the business plan identify issues of strategic concern to the organization?

Often, workplace health promotion programs are created and implemented without proper consideration of these emerging issues. Some programs will likely fail and have failed simply because they have not addressed this changing work ethic. It is important to recognize three categories of mistakes that can lead to failure..

Organizational--These are problems outside the control, but not the influence of employees. These problems are caused primarily by insufficient job design, improper work tasks, lack of supervision, insufficient administration, inadequate training, and lack of career development.

Program--These problems relate to mistakes made in the planning, design, and implementation of the program.

People--These problems relate to the nature of program support by top management, the values and norms in the organizational climate, degree of support among participants, degree of interpersonal conflict in the organization, and of competency of program facilitators.

Health promotion should not be viewed as a panacea for all organizational and people problems. However, HP programs do offer some predictable and beneficial payoffs, but they will only be successful in improving health and work productivity if employers recognize that the organizational system and climate must support the health promotion intervention.

NEEDS ASSESSMENT TIME LINE

The following four week time line is somewhat arbitrary, but can be useful in planning HP efforts. The "C" in the graph below indicates an activity conducted by a Consultant or a Coordinator. The "O" refers to activities conducted by the Organization. The time line can be a useful tool to plan your program and to coordinate various activities throughout. You may want to use a large erasable wall calendar that covers a several month period.These calendars provide "the big picture," and can be used as a visual aid by your task team to plan and schedule people, materials, and meeting rooms from the very beginning.

Needs Assessment Time Line

	Week Number			
Activity	1	2	3	4
Initial contact	C,O			
Advance survey sent out	C			
Data gathered by company	O>>>>>>>>>>>>O			
Advance survey results meeting		C,O		
Questionnaires/Site visit			C,O	
Interviews			C,O	
Analysis of data and preparation of Summary Report			C>>>>>>>>>>>>>>>C	
Presentation of Summary Report				C,O

THE TASK FORCE AND COMMITTEE PLANNING

Forming a task force committee to plan the health promotion effort is imperative. Not only is it helpful in building a consensus within the organization, but when operated correctly, the committee member's involvement will nurture a feeling of "ownership" in the program. You can plan the perfect program based on organizational and individual needs, yet see the effort fail because the employees had no stake in the outcome. The following steps provide simply one framework for a more open, proactive planning process.

STEP ONE: Get Upper Management Mandate and Support. This is the one step that must take place before the Task Force is actually organized. Ideally, upper management support should come in a number of important forms. These may include:

1. Commitment of resources (Money, time, and power).
2. Personal participation in program.
3. Commitment to a healthy work environment.
4. Providing access to communication channels.
5. Making Statement of Purpose for the health promotion benefit to all employees.

STEP TWO: Choose A Task Planning Committee. A team of motivated, concerned and well-respected employees for program planning is imperative to your program's success. An employee team helps ensure employee "ownership" of the program which enhances employee commitment and participation. Also, the team approach ensures advice and direction and continuation of the program despite personnel changes. All levels of employees, management and non-management, should be represented on this important committee. Although no hard and fast rules apply as to the exact number of committee members, six to ten is usually considered an optimum size. Here is one example of a composition for this committee:

1. Health Promotion Facilitator/Consultant.
2. Representative of Upper Management.
3. Training Manage.r
4. Human Resource Manager.
5. Safety Representative.
6. Middle Manager (Supervisor).
7. Employees without supervisory duties (at least two line employees.
8. Employee Relations Manager.

There may be other employee categories that you would want on your planning committee. In small organizations do not worry about the titles of the departments solicited, just invite those important for program development and success. Some examples of other types of committees that might be used as allies include a smoking policy committee, a child care committee, a food and nutrition committee, and a fitness committee.

Qualities of Task Force Members--Try to get people involved who are respected for their competence and who are also enthusiastic supporters of wellness. Ideally, you want your task force members to have the following qualities:

1. An interest in health.
2. A healthy lifestyle.
3. Leadership and/or credibility among other employees.
4. Access to, or respected by, top management.

Providing Incentives To Committee Members--You may need to main-tain the motivation and interest of the committee members. The following incentives may be useful:

1. Time off from regular work for committee duties.
2. Special social gatherings for the group.
3. Outside visitation to other programs.
4. Preview of program materials and content.

STEP THREE: Clarifying Goals and Objectives. Every plan must start with a statement of mission, goals and objectives. Since the needs and interests of the organization may not mirror those of the individual employee, the potential for conflict and disunity are present. All other factors being equal, the closer the program comes to matching the organization's goals and objectives with the employees' needs and interests, the more successful the program will be. The following steps may be helpful in the goal-planning process.

Health Promotion Mission and Goals--An example of a mission statement might be: "To create a corporate culture that contains health care costs by improving the overall health of the workforce." Another example might be: "To improve the productivity of the workforce by involving them in health promotion activities that are designed to increase morale and reduce absenteeism through better management practices, exercise and stress reduction." Another is to provide a better balance between personal and organizational health and productivity." Program goals are more specific. The following list of goals are representative.

___	Increased productivity
___	Increased morale
___	Decreased absenteeism
___	Improved company image
___	Improved employee/employer relations
___	Decreased turnover
___	Decreased health care costs
___	Decreased life insurance costs
___	Fewer Worker's Compensation claims
___	Other_____

Other key management personnel will also have their ideas concerning organizational goals. This input is extremely useful. However, we caution that before you establish the goals and objectives for your program that you also evaluate the needs and interests of the individual employees. The purpose of clarifying the mission and goals is to give the program direction and meaning. These goals should not be fixed in concrete, and although set early in the planning process, they should also be constantly reviewed. Some goals can have short-term considerations, while others will likely take years to accomplish.

Employee Needs and Interests--Two factors can be used to help determine what the employees want and what they need, which are not always the same. Initially, the data obtained from the Needs and Interest Survey can provide a subjective appraisal. Input can also be obtained from the Health Risk Appraisal. Additional informal surveys and interviews can be conducted by committee members. Talk to everyone possible and solicit their ideas, comments, support, and help.

STEP FOUR--Program Planning. A business plan or proposal is a comprehensive statement of the monetary, and non-monetary activities, resources, procedures, that answers the following questions: Who? What? Where, When? How? How Much? To consider any attempt to achieve the desired outcome without considering the activities resources needed to pursue the desired course of action is meaningless. There are two general categories of resources, activities and procedures: company resources and people resources. The following is an example of a resource list that will assist you in planning activities:

THE RESOURCE LIST

I. **Company Resources**
   1. TIME (When will the group sessions be held?)
      A. Company time for salaried workers.
      B. Lunchtime and before and after work for hourly workers if a union is not involved.

   2. SPACE (Where will the participants meet?)
      A. Conference room during, before, and after work--Holds 35 people.
      B. Outside area allows for walking and jogging during nice weather.

   3. EQUIPMENT (What materials will be used?)
      A. Use of TV and VCR from training department.
      B. Use of copier and word processor for preparing materials.

   4. EXISTING PROGRAMS (What do we have in place that we can use to support our program--Newsletter, EAP?)
      A. Employee newsletter can present health articles and announce events.
      B. Cafeteria can start featuring healthier food choices.

II. **People Resources**
   1. Plant nurse is a CPR instructor and can speak on health topics
   2. New line worker is a certified aerobic instructor.
   3. Upper management (CEO in particular) is a strong wellness advocate.
   4. Several employees are experts in a number of wellness areas; nutrition, exercise, and stress management.
   5. Two people with good organizational skills have volunteered their services to help with logistics.

Next, one must organize the information and data about employee interest and health practices. Activities and topics are suggested by areas of broad concern and repeated responses on items of need or interest. For example workshops on the topics of smoking, fitness, stress reduction, weight management, how to reduce health risks, creating a life-long wellness lifestyle.

STEP FIVE--Decide on Activities and Promotion/ Marketing Strategies.
This step involves the decisions about what we will finally offer, how do we get the word out about the program, and how do we proceed in a way that will

encourage our employees to want to participate? The types of activities can be prioritized after we've listed them and then we can solicit input from our health promotion committee and all concerned parties. Use the data gathered from the various surveys or, if you are a consultant trying to submit a proposal bid, refer to the request for proposal (RFP) The major issues to consider in this step, as they relate to maximizing participation are:

1. **The product**--what will we deliver, what is feasible, what is a priority for various segments of employees?
2. **The price/cost/incentives**--How much will it cost from both employees' and companies viewpoint: or will it be free or take up too much time or is it a priority without me knowing how it will benefit me? What are the educational, financial, interpersonal, policy and public relations costs, benefits and possible incentives?
3. **The promotion**--What will we say about our program, and through what means will we say it? How will we present the product so the right people will be likely to use it? These issues will be covered in much greater detail in our discussion on promotion and marketing.

STEP SIX--Devise a Preliminary Budget & Financial Plan. The key categories are salaries and benefits (whether full-time program manager or limited number of hours allocated from numerous employees in the human resources, training, employee relations or medical departments), outside consultants, supplies, marketing expenses, communications/media, travel, space/facilities, equipment, cost associated with participation, and overhead. Distinguish between development (consultants) and operating costs because the former should occur only once. Sources of funding to meet development and operating expenses can come from grants, program fees, cost-sharing (employees and employer contributing) health cost savings, options in cafeteria-style benefits package, arrangement with insurance company to reduce premiums contingent upon reduced claims experience, savings resulting from reducing turnover, absenteeism and other related expenses, and even potential income as a consulting profit center.

STEP SEVEN--Devise a Preliminary Evaluation Plan. Even though evaluations are done at programs' end, they must be planned at this point to have any meaning. We will want to gather data on an on-going basis so that we know how employees react to and feel about the programs, and to measure what impact have the components of the program had on the organization. Determining at this point what possible measurements might be used to measure improvement and success will help in designing evaluation instruments that will ask the right questions. Evaluation will be discussed in further detail in a later chapter.

STEP EIGHT--Develop The Short Term Plan. One of the early tasks of the task force committee is to decide when and how to begin the program. This strategy must take into account the factors we have mentioned in the previous steps. The plan should be a written one that includes:

1. Objective statement for each of the company goals.
2. Selection of program intensity. (Will the beginning components be designed to primarily educate, or actually to affect behavior changes?)
3. Decide on a time frame for implementation.
4. Select the ways to promote and communicate the relevant information.
5. Plan program logistics.

An Outline For a First Committee Meeting--No hard and fast rule exists for how these committee meetings should be structured. Organizations should use a style that has worked for them in other contexts. With the coordinator acting as group facilitator, here is one model that has been used successfully:

1. Introductions/Icebreaker.
2. Statement of purpose (mission statement).
3. Facilitator explains basic concept of wellness and health promotion.
4. Goals for program are discussed.
5. Basic timetable for committee tasks is discussed.
6. Discussion period (obstacles, corporate culture, interests of group)
7. Committee members are provided with survey forms to obtain feedback.
8. Statement of intent to implement a program and a solicitation of support/feedback can come from this first meeting.

The Flow Chart- Organization health promotion programs vary in their structure and scope. The following flowchart provides just one way of mapping the long-term path of the overall effort. While the sequence of events shown in this diagram seem to have a logical order, in fact they have a great deal of overlap. Planning, for instance, continues throughout the entire program, while evaluation must begin in the planning stage and is perpetual.

Sample Flow Chart for Implementation
of a Health Promotion Program

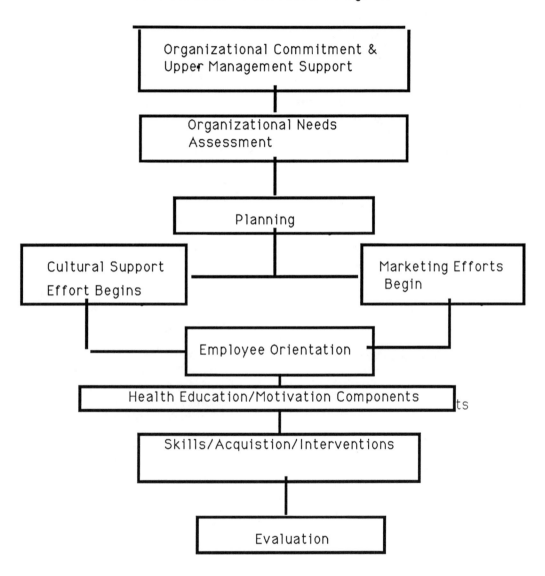

LOGICAL STEPS IN A PROGRAM DEVELOPMENT

Step 1:   Identification of a health problem in the workplace.

• Cigarette smoking

Step 2:   Number of employees who experience the problem.

• Approximately 28% of the workforce

Step 3:   Number of employees program is intended to reach.

• The program is intended to reach all smokers in the workplace.

Step 4:   Number who actually attend the program.

• We'd consider our marketing efforts successful if 25%of the total smoking population attended the introductory meeting and 20% began the program.

Step 5:   Number who learn skills and obtain relevant information.

• #_____

Step 6:   Number who begin practicing new behavior patterns.

• If 15% of the smoking population achieved Steps 5 & 6, we would feel "on target."

Step 7:   Number who sustain behavior change over a given time frame.

We would need a one-year success rate of 50% in order to achieve our goal of reducing the smoking population by 10% in one year. (While this is high for community HP programs, many work-site programs exceed this figure.

Step 8:   Number for whom practice of the behaviors is linked to improved physiological and psychological status.

• Most new non-smokers report positive changes in their health. Tracking health care utilization could provide a statistical link between quitting and improved personal health.

Step 9:   Reduction in morbidity and mortality risk.

• This can be shown prospectively by comparing Before-and-After Health Risk Appraisals.

Step 10:   Achievement of organizational objective(s).

- Tangible ones include reduction in health care costs, reduction in absenteeism, and lower turnover.

- Less tangible and difficult to measure are improved employee/employer relations, increased productivity, and less stressful work environment.

6

STARTING AND DEVELOPING SUCCESSFUL PROGRAMS

INTRODUCTION

The goal of the program development and implementation phase is to make a smooth and successful transition from the plan to the fully operating program. Although we have covered some dimensions of implementation in the last chapter we will explore issues that will assist us to keep the health promotion program from fading into the organizational woodwork. An effectively-managed implementation strategy is as important to the overall success of the program as the program plan itself.

THE START-UP PHASE

Ask yourself the following five questions to serve as a guide to planning the start-up of the program phase.

ONE: Which program component needs to be begun first? Your answer to this question will be derived from the data gathered during the planning stage. For example, we will select smoking cessation as one of the programs to be implemented, which will allow us to address the four issues in step two.

TWO: What are the development steps required to successfully implement each component?

A. **Determine the level of need and interest in the program.**
   This is also an issue that is often decided in the planning stage. Employee surveys can help answer the pertinent questions, i.e, do we have enough interest to begin a smoking cessation program?

B. **Examine program options and choose one.**
   Which stop-smoking program will we provide? Will one with a higher success rate and higher costsbetter suit our needs one that is lower in both success rate and cost?

C. **Plan program development features.**
   Dates, times, manpower, and budget are key issues. Timing is especially important. From our experience the best time to start a smoking cessation is in January after people have celebrated the holidays and have made their New Year's resolutions. The worst time is in December while people are experiencing the stress and demands of the holiday season.

D. **Begin promotional and marketing efforts and introduce the program.**
   This step continues until program is implemented. Marketing may include articles in newsletter concerning harmful effects of smoking, and/or announcement of upcoming program. Brochures, flyers, bulletin board announcements, announcements at meetings and memos from CEO and senior level supporters are also considerations. An introductory meeting where employee can meet with program presenters and hear about the program in a non-pressure environment. Remember to use more than one media to get your message across. Also use a common theme and create a program logo thta will be instantly recognized and linked with your program.

E. **Begin the program.**
   If the other steps are done correctly, this one should not present last minute surprises and problems.

THREE: What are the major timetables for each of the sub-steps mentioned in item two? The following is a timeline one might use for start-up of a smoking cessation program,counting backward from your planned start date:

FOUR MONTHS BEFORE: Determine level of need and interest in a particular program.
THREE MONTHS BEFORE: Examine program options and choose several.
TWO MONTHS BEFORE: Plan program implementation techniques.
ONE MONTH BEFORE: Begin promotion and marketing efforts and introduce program.
DAY ZERO: Program begins.

FOUR: What support and financial resources, including funding, space, technological assistance, and people are required for each step? This step addresses such issues as follows:

A. Will our program provide incentives and rewards?
B. Where will the class be held and at what time of day?
C. What support staff will be needed for implementation?
D. What will the marketing effort include?

FIVE: What will be the measures of success? What criteria will be used to determine individual success in this program? What additional criteria will be used to measure organizational success? For example, when a program participant quits smoking and remains so for a period of one year, he/she will be considered a success for the purpose of measurement. If this success results in a significant reduction in absenteeism and health care claims costs for the group as a whole, then the program will be considered successful.

CHARACTERISTICS OF SUCCESSFUL HP ACTIVITIES

What common features are seen in behavior change programs that achieve successful results? Good health and effective behavior come in all shapes and sizes. We will discuss some differences in a later segment of this chapter.Not all of the aspects described here are present in successful lifestyle change programs, but many are. Below are some aspects we have identified as important. This list is not definitive and you may have others to add.

One-to-one interaction--Although this is not a common feature of workplace wellness programs, many of the best programs--those that have the greatest impact on participants--seem to support a high level of personal interaction. In the case of assessment programs (i.e., Health Risk Appraisals, Fitness Testing, e.g.), this is important for motivational and educational reasons. In behavior change programs, personal interaction with a health professional or program presenter can provide valuable feedback and at the same time transmit an "I care" feeling.

Group support--Many researchers *(Brownell and Felix, 1987)* feel that group support is necessary for maintenance of major lifestyle changes. Supportive environments away from the workplace are imperative for maintenance of long-term lifestyle changes. As noted in chapter one, the built-in support system provided by the work environment is one of the reasons long-term success rates are higher for workplace programs.

Follow-up--For programs where medical compliance is a major issue, diabetes and hypertension, among others, the importance of follow-up is clearly documented. Program components have a clear beginning and an ending. However, in instances where health professionals or HP coordinators take the time to follow up, the anecdotal evidence seems highly favorable. Consider the employee who is recognized and rewarded at the end of one year for sustaining a major behavior change.

Upper management support--This was discussed earlier and will not be elaborated on here except to say that where upper management is involved in a positive way--through participation, recognition, and reward giving--health promotion is usually interpreted as a positive employee benefit.

Voluntary participation--Not only is this a characteristic of a successful program, along with confidentiality, it is a necessary condition. With the exception of safety programs that are enacted to meet OSHA requirements (and possibly a few other exceptions), participation in a wellness program must be voluntary. One cornerstone of organizational health promotion is personal responsibility, and when participation is mandated, a vital ingredient necessary for personal growth is missing.

Confidentiality--All manner of problems arise, including legal ones, when confidentiality is compromised. Health promotion managers and consultants need not only take every precaution to ensure that privacy is protected, but they must clearly communicate this to prospective participants. Unless otherwise told, many employees will assume that written records will be available to supervisors or upper managers. A few people may remain unconvinced even when told that all information is confidential so you may need to explain how this procedure is actually done to insure privacy.

A PROGRAM MODEL

As we discuss these steps and follow the example of a smoking cessation program, think how another health promotion program might also fit these steps (stress, weight control, etc.).

STEP ONE: Understand Your Culture. Our cultures tend to have a very strong negative impact upon our health practices. If we wish to change and to maintain health changes for any length of time, we need to become aware of this impact and to arrange our lives in such a way that the negative influences are minimal and positive influences are substituted for them. Using the example of a smoking cessation program, Step One would ask the smoker to investigate some of the environmental factors that influence his/her smoking habit and develop a strategy for minimizing them.

STEP TWO: Get the Facts and Separate Fact from Fiction. There are two kinds of facts that are of interest in a health promotion program. One involves the health information that is necessary to plan a program of change; the second involves the facts about ourselves that we will need to apply to our own lives. In this one step, we can combine personal assessment with health education. For example, a smoker would obtain increased knowledge about smoking and discover some of the reasons why he or she smokes.

STEP THREE: Create and Build Supportive Environments. Before any plan is started, it is critical to create a supportive environment in which the plan has a reasonable chance of success. If this is not done, the best programs are likely to fail. With a supportive environment, even the weakest programs have some chance for success. We might use an "adopt a smoker" program and enlist family support. One of the most important elements in creating a supportive environment is to build effective support groups that will help achieve our objectives in a change program. The mutual support of others with the same problem is probably one of the strongest arguments favoring stop smoking classes. Time spent with others learning to cope with life after smoking is a key aspect of most all cessation programs. In addition to support groups, we alter other aspects of our environment, such as modifying our schedules, redefining our centers of interest and trying to change the organization's policy to support nonsmoking.

STEP FOUR: Put Your Plan Into Action. If you have systematically followed the first three steps, then the fourth step will follow as a completely free choice. The objectives will be to choose your own rather than someone else's vision of what you "should" or "shouldn't" do. You need to decide just what level of commitment you are ready to make. Without a commitment based on your own free choice, very little will be accomplished. When it is your own decision, you can create much more success. Apply the strategies and techniques that will make you personally successful. If you always lit up a cigarette whenever you experienced stress, you will need to develop and practice a new behavior for these difficult moments.

STEP FIVE: Be Aware of How You Feel. In this step, you tune in to how you feel when you overeat, overdrink, are tense and anxious; and then compare that to how you feel when you have exercised, eaten nutritiously, or stayed relaxed. And as you stop smoking or start running, you will tune in to how much better your body feels. Additionally, keep a record of how you are doing. How much trimmer is your waist? How much better do you feel? This feedback about your progress acts as a spur to further action. For instance, when smokers quit, they often quickly experience positive physical benefits. Those who focus on these positive changes seem to have the easiest time getting through the short-term withdrawal phase.

STEP SIX: Reward Yourself and Have Fun. No change is going to continue unless it is rewarding in terms of fun, satisfaction, recognition, status, material rewards, or the enjoyment you are having with others in your program. You need to feel good about the change you are making. This step allows you to invent and plan rewards for yourself right from the very beginning, as soon as you complete the first step toward change. And, if you succeed in your plan, then you deserve a reward. Successful participants in a smoking cessation program focus on the rewards of being a nonsmoker.

STEP SEVEN: Reach Out To Others. This step asks you to reach out to others, because just as you need the help of others to achieve your goals, others may need help from you in order to achieve their own goals. Once you achieve some success then you are in a unique position to help others. Though often branded "new converts" or "zealots" by their still-smoking friends and relatives, new non-smokers exert a strong positive influence on them by planting the idea, "If they can do it, maybe I can too!" Helping others who share your goals reinforces your own behavior, and thus you are more likely to benefit from the program and maintain your gains. We cannot over-emphasize the importance of maintaining support systems when making lifestyle changes. This fact is supported by data on the recidivism rate for both personal and organizational programs.

WORKPLACE COMPETITIONS: THE NEWEST WRINKLE THAT FOSTERS CULTURAL SUPPORT

Workplace competitions or contests have been recently utilized to maximize the effectiveness of health promotion programs. Such competitions typically involve contests between groups to see who can lose the most weight, make the greatest increases in numbers of work teams who exercise, stop smoking in the greatest numbers, etc. The first published evaluation of a health promotion competition appeared in 1984 *(Brownell and Felix,1987)*. In the years since, many programs based on competition have been implemented.

Brownell reports that there is a growing emphasis on *how* a program is delivered, as well as the traditional health education program's focus on *what* information is delivered. The how issue is related to the need to build and sustain motivation. Research has shown a consistent relationship between social support and health. Cooperation between individuals united by a cause underlies movements ranging from national patriotism to team sports. According to *Brownell*, competition between groups can enhance cooperation between individual members of each group, thereby strengthening the social support available to each individual. These are briefly summarized below.

Weight Control--In his own studies, *Brownell* has demonstrated that the cost-per-pound-lost for the workplace competition program was considerably less than with other more commonly used methods for weight loss. In one study, the competitive situation resulted in a cost-per-pound-lost of $2.93, whereas a non-competitive University Clinic program delivered at the workplace resulted in a cost-per-pound-lost of $44.60.

Smoking Cessation Programs--In one recent study of a workplace competition for smoking cessation, the results showed that 18% of the smokers stopped in a program based almost entirely on competition, while only 7% quit in a control group that was provided a standard 6-week cognitive-behavioral program.

Exercise Programs--Very few of these programs using competitions have been evaluated, but the anecdotal evidence seems to indicate much greater participation when competitions are implemented.

Competitions in the workplace to promote healthier lifestyles are the wave of the future. Brownell's research has inspired other thoughtful educators, and health professionals to move beyond program content to explore the organizational dynamics that inspire individual motivation and success.

CATEGORIES OF HEALTH PROMOTION ACTIVITIES

Here are some general categories of HP activities currently provided to organizational settings. Be aware that these categories are not mutually exclusive. Some of this section should actually be a review of materials already discussed. For example, most good programs are likely to include some elements from all of the categories. You will notice the similarities of these categories to the model for developing personal wellness programs. Throughout this section on health promotion activities, we will highlight key programs and present summaries of start-up characteristics and strategies.

ASSESSMENTS

Activities in this area are designed to help the individual participant determine the current state of their health and aspects of it in need of change. These assessments may measure a wide spectrum of health variables or they may focus on one specific area. A good example of a multi-dimensional assessment is the Health Risk Appraisal. An example of single dimensional assessment is a blood pressure, cholesterol, body fat, diet or fitness analysis. Below are listed a number of these assessments:

1. Wellness inventories
2. Fitness evaluations
3. Hypertension screening (Example #1 below)
4. Nutrition evaluation
5. Yearly physical
6. Health Risk Appraisal (Example #2 below)

HYPERTENSION SCREENING

Definition of a Hypertension Screening Program: Blood pressure (BP) is the force on the walls of the blood vessels as the blood flows through. A single elevated reading does not constitute a diagnosis of high blood pressure (HBP), but is a sign that further evaluation is needed. Systolic is the pressure in the walls of the blood vessels as the heart beats, and diastolic is the pressure in the vessels when the heart is at rest, between beats. A person with chronically high blood pressure (HBP) is said to have hypertension. HBP is defined by most clinicians as either a systolic reading of above 140 or a diastolic pressure reading of above 90, or both of these conditions. A normal reading is said to be around 120/80. Physician referral is usually indicated when any of the three HBP conditions above are present. A workplace hypertension screening program is an organized effort to educate, detect, refer, and follow-up those individuals at risk for this disease.

Incidence of HBP in the Workplace Population--Some studies have indicated that as many as 30% of the workforce may be experiencing High Blood Pressure at any one time. Other, more conservative estimates place the incidence at 25%. The most insidious aspect of these numbers relates to the vast number of people who do not know they have the chronic condition. Hypertension is known as the silent killer, since it usually has no symptoms. Over time, hypertension results in weakening of the blood vessels, and places more strain on the heart and kidneys, which in turn can lead to heart failure, stroke, or kidney disease. The disease of hypertension is the major risk factor for stroke--the third leading cause of death in the U.S., and a leading risk factor for heart disease, the number one cause of premature death.

Characteristics Of Hypertension Screening Programs

Education--The employee is informed what HBP is, the risks of untreated HBP, the benefits and necessity of following prescribed treatment, and the availability of the workplace program. Education is presented concerning the relationship between high blood pressure and poor stress managemen.

Detection--The BP of participating employees is taken to identify those with HBP.

Referral--The employee with an above normal BP reading is referred to medical care resource in his community for evaluation and possible treatment.

Follow-up--The employee is contacted at regular intervals to be sure that he or she obtained medical help and to monitor progress in therapy, as well as to reinforce patient education.

Quality Control Issues

Below are examples of some of the quality control issues for ensuring the success of a worksite blood pressure control program. The following questions should be asked and satisfactorily answered:

1. Is personnel trained and/or credentialed?
2. Will they provide re-checks?
3. Do they conduct follow-ups to assure that medical evaluations occurred?
4. Do they provide an education/motivation component?
5. How is confidentiality of records assured?

Design And Cost Considerations

This is one of the easier components to consider since it only requires one trained professional, usually a registered nurse. Also required is a small, private area such as an office. The key elements of success are accurate record keeping, confidentiality, and follow-up by the professional.

The education component, ideally targeted to entire workforce--newsletter articles, flyers, posters, etc.--can serve as a key marketing tool to get as many workers involved as possible. It follows that the more people who participate in the initial screening, the more high-risk workers you will identify.

It is important to note that in the first year after start-up, health care costs for the employer are likely to rise, since referred hypertensive employees file medical claims. Many are followed-up long-term by their physician, and many of these may take medication for the rest of their lives. Harder to calculate is the lowered incidence of disease and death resulting from long-term control of this disease.

A COMPREHENSIVE HEALTH PROMOTION EVENT

When used in its most optimum way, any program can become the springboard from which a comprehensive wellness program can be launched. We have described below features of an activity that may provide this foundation for a workplace program.

Marketing and Promotion--An advertising piece is provided to each member of the target workforce population. Use other marketing techniques (posters, health promotion employee brochure, newsletter story, etc.) as indicate for re-inforcing your message. The timing of any promotion is important and may be linked to the pace of activity in the culture. For example, promotion done too early in a fast paced organization may be forgotten.

The Initial Medical And Fitness Screening--A one-to-one appointment with a program representative is conducted before or immediately after the work day and takes approximately 45-60 minutes. The participant also fills out a health questionnaire and a nurse or doctor can take various health data readings-- blood pressure, draws a blood sample, tests for body fat content, the employee's height. The range of tests conducted are dependent upon the type of program and situation of the participant. This appointment is voluntary and confidential, with each participant receiving a coded ID number. The staff invites the participating employee to the follow-up interpretive session.

The Interpretive Session--This session occurs approximately two to three weeks after the initial appointment. The participants are introduced to the concept of wellness, the data from the test is evaluated, various components and classes in the program are discussed, and general questions are answered. Any "high risk" participant is strongly urged to schedule an individual follow-up appointments with the health professionals. .

Written Wellness Materials Or Guidebook--Each participant is provided initial program materials highlighting most of the following areas:

    A.   A narrative introduction to and discussion of wellness as a positive lifestyle alternative.
    B.   Feedback information from the testing.
    C.   A detailed explanation concerning how to interpret the results.
    D.   Information on how to reduce lifestyle risk factors.
    E.   A wellness inventory that will help the participant identify other issues related to health and well-being.
    F.   A module on how to build and sustain motivation when making lifestyle changes.
    G.   A strategy for setting personal goals for health and well-being.

Individual Consultations-- Confidential questions can be answered as rapport is established between the employee and the health promotion and medical professionals during 15 to 20 minute sessions throughout the program. Goals are reviewed and the participant is directed to the most relevant health promotion activities. Community and supplemental resources are recommended where appropriate.

Summary Reports--The organization can receive various summary reports that identify risks in the portion of the workforce indicated from various tests and questionnaires. This is only reports numbers in summary fashion that protects the confidentiality of all participants.

The Six Month or One year Post-Test--A one year post-test is recommended to measure organizational and individual effectiveness of the overall health promotion program. A subjective questionnaire that measures employee attitudes will also be administered.

The Evaluation--Relevant data at one year can provide indicators concerning program effectiveness--its strengths and weaknesses. Individual progress can be assessed and lifestyle changes, individual and organizational, can be rewarded, if appropriate. Medical cost care data can be assessed and compared to establish relationships and trends.

EDUCATION AND MOTIVATION

Every health promotion professional faces the reality that not every employee is ready or willing to make lifestyle changes at the precise moment a given wellness effort is presented. Educational components of a wellness program are most effectively used as a first introduction to a key program area of health promotion and wellness. Many employees lack crucial knowledge about their own negative health behaviors or habit patterns, as well as general knowledge of the health promotion subjects. The goal of these activities is to educate and to motivate. This should be clearly understood so that educational efforts will not be confused with specific program efforts. However, it should be noted that some participants in these efforts will need only the education in order to make the necessary lifestyle change. Due to cost and time constraints faced by organizations in pursuit of their primary goals, these educational activities are often used as a "trade-off." This is not the preferred approach to use, but is better than no program at all. Some of the more successful start-up educational programs are listed below:

1. HRA interpretations. (Too many HRA programs stop here.)
2. Wellness lectures. (Usually one-hour lunch sessions called "Brown Bags.")
3. Back injury prevention education.
4. Nutrition education.
5. Alcohol/drug awareness. (Can be one component of an EAP.)
6. Health fairs.

7. Newsletters.
8. Proper use of health care resources and benefits.
9. Workplace safety. (lifting, CPR, first aid, defensive driving)
10. Behavioral change programs.

BEHAVIOR CHANGE PROGRAMS

Well-conceived, behavior change programs contain elements that assess behavior and attitudes in certain lifestyle areas, provide education and motivation, opportunities to learn and practice new behavioral skills, and include the cultural supports essential to sustain the new behaviors. Such programs also offer the best chance for permanent lifestyle change. Among the most common of these offered in workplace settings are the following:

1. Stress Management
2. Cardiovascular Fitness
3. Smoking Cessation
4. Weight Management
5. Nutritional Management
6. Self-care skills (BP monitoring, selecting a physician, buying generic drugs, recognition of warning signs, communication with health care providers)

SMOKING CESSATION PROGRAMS

The latest survey by the American Cancer Society reveals that about 26% of U.S. adults smoke cigarettes. The average work-force will have about this same percentage. However, only a portion of them will want to quit at the exact time a program is started and/or want to use a formal stop smoking program. Cigarette smoking is the single largest preventable cause of death in the United States, conservatively killing 350,000 people each year. Regular use of cigarettes has been shown to result in an increased likelihood of many fatal conditions, including heart disease and cancer, the two leading causing of death in the U.S. Because the risks due to cigarette smoking are reversible by quitting smoking, this premature death and disease is preventable. Smokers who quit and remain off cigarettes also tend to positively change other health-related behaviors such as nutrition and exercise.

Workplace stop smoking programs can benefit the employer and the employee. The workplace offers a setting where social support can be used or built to improve capabilities for making these difficult lifestyle changes. Workers benefit by having accessibility to programs designed to meet their needs. Programs often have positive effects on job satisfaction and employee morale. In the long-run, employees may also see reductions in personal health care costs. Certain workers, by the nature of their current or past jobs, may be at particularly high risk for smoking related illnesses.

Practical advantages of workplace stop smoking programs include the convenience for participation, the use of established information and communication networks both formal and informal, and the increased likelihood of long-term success. Workplace sponsored smoking cessation programs often benefit the organization by potential reductions in health care costs, reductions in absenteeism and turnover, and increases in employee coping capabilities and productivity.

EXAMPLE OF A SMOKING CESSATION PROGRAM

The following material consists of excerpts taken from a training manual for a smoking cessation program titled, ONCE & FOR ALL. This program has been developed by the authors for use in a number of organizational settings.

ONCE & FOR ALL! (O&FA!)

O&FA! is a group program designed to help aspiring non-smokers deal with all aspects of the smoking problem: emotional, addictive, and habitual. The program helps each smoker build and sustain motivation to quit, and change attitudes and habits inconsistent with being a non-smoker. Participants in the program learn positive replacement habits as they quit. Quitting usually is not the difficult part for most aspiring non-smokers--remaining smoke free is. The program guides participanst through the crucial readjustment period and strives to help them discover the true pleasure of not smoking. Long term abstinence is then the likely result. The program can be broken down into four phases as follows:

Phase 1: Introductory (Sales) Session. Prospective participants gather information about the program and if they decide to enroll they are given booklet titled, "The First 5 Days." They begin using this booklet five days before the first treatment session.

Phase 2: Five consecutive daily group sessions. This is the cessation phase, the time when most participants who become non-smokers actually quit smoking.

Phase 3: The follow-up sessions. This consists of several sessions to help new non-smokers (and aspiring new non-smokers) adjust to life without cigarettes.

Phase 4: Long-term support sessions. We help organize and provide some of the resource material for bi-monthly, self-help meetings where participants discuss anything related to quitting smoking.

Program Goals--The following are the goals of the O&FA program:

1. To significantly reduce the number of employees who smoke.
2. To teach replacement skills and positive habits to employees who wish to quit.
3. To provide a supportive, nurturing environment for smokers who attempt to quit.
4. To contribute to an improvement in the indoor air quality of the workplace.

Program Guidelines--This program adheres to the quality control guidelines of the "Code of Practice for Smoking Cessation Programs" set by the Peer Review Committee on National Smoking Cessation. In summary, these guidelines state the following:

1. Complete cessation, and continued abstinence from smoking for one year should be the primary criteria for success.
2. Program should be tailored to needs, background, environment, social needs, of family and peer support, and health problems.
3. Should include skill building through behavior change practices as part of the program.
4. Should include a weight control/stress management and/or exercise component.
5. Should increase understanding by employees of the health benefits of quitting.
6. Should not emphasize scare tactics.
7. For people with special health problems, program should coordinate with participants' physicians.
8. Should provide for referral of participants who did not respond to treatment to alternative programs.
9. Should be able to offer assistance to participants in establishing a maintenance support component to continue after the formal program is finished.
10. Should provide some alternatives for people who are, for whatever reason, not yet ready to quit.

Program Learning Objectives--As a result of attending this program, participants will obtain:
1. Skills in understanding and modifying the factors that led to and perpetuated the maintenance of a smoker's habit (i.e., peer pressure, quantity per day, habituation, and addiction).
2. An understanding of the relationship of new behavior after quitting to health and well-being and the relationship of smoking to chronic diseases.
3. Skills in the use of an effective stop smoking method that can potentially work for each person. Individual differences should be accommodated.
4. Skills necessary to maintain new, non-smoking behavior and lifestyle.
5. Skills for practicing stress reduction/relaxation techniques.
6. An awareness of additional resources and support systems.

How To Measure And Evaluate Success Rates--The criteria for measuring success rate must be uniform in any good program. Credibility for any effective stop smoking program can only be obtained when we conform to the generally accepted evaluation standards for smoking cessation programs. The following definitions and guidelines for measuring success have been set for our program with these standards in mind.

Smoker--Any person who smokes tobacco in any form.

Participant--Any smoker who attends at least the first treatment session following orientation.

Dropout--Any participant who does not complete the program.

Attrition Rate--Number of dropouts divided by the number of participants.

Short Term Success--Any participant who has completed the program and stopped smoking by the end of the program.

Long Term Success--Any short term successful client who has not resumed smoking for at least one year after completion of the program.

Overall Success--Any participant who has not resumed smoking for at least one year after completion of the program.

Recidivist--Participant who stopped smoking by the end of the program, but resumed during the ensuing 12 months.

Success Measurements--The standard definition of success in smoking cessation programs is complete abstention from smoking tobacco in any form (and substituting any other form of tobacco in its place) for at least one year after completion of the pro-gram. Other measures are sometimes reported to indicate program impact on participants, i.e., switching to pipes or cigars, switching from high to low-tar/nicotine cigarettes, abstention for less than one year, and reduction in consumption rate. However, for the purpose of collecting and reporting program cessation rate only "Long Term Success" as defined above should be used. The most important data for measuring success rate includes the following for each stop smoking group:

1. The total number of participants.
2. The number of smokers who stopped smoking at the end of the program.
3. The number of smokers completing the program who have not resumed smoking at the end of one year.
4. Attendance record for each participant.
5. Documentation of baseline tobacco behavior, at completion of program, and at end of one year.
6. Personal data for purposes of phone follow-up and/or mailed questionnaire. Collecting this information is vital since by the conservative standards we apply to the analysis of the success rate, all those who we fail to reach must be counted as smokers. This is an assumption that is warranted by the experience of many studies.

Formulas For Calculating Success Rates

Attrition Rate = dropouts + those still smoking at end of program | by participants.

Short-Term Success Rate = those who have quit smoking at conclusion of program | by participants.

Long-Term Success Rate = those who have completed program and have not smoked for a year | by those who have quit smoking at the end of the program (short-term success).

Overall Success Rate = those who have completed program and have not smoked for a year | by the total number of participants.

Note that the first three definitions do not take dropouts into accoun. Many programs that meet once a week from the beginning of their program, have a high dropout rate. Smokers are not asked to quit until the fourth or fifth week in these programs. By not taking these dropouts into account, the one year (long-term) success rate is artificially high. We believe that the most relevant statistic is the overall success rate that takes total number of participants into account. If someone representing another program tells you that their long-term success rate is 50%, but their dropout rate is 50%, then their overall success rate is 25%.

Attitude Questionnaire. The following two questionnaires are designed to provide feedback to the instructor and to the smoker concerning smoking attitudes and behaviors.

What are Your Attitudes Toward Quitting Smoking?

(If you are a smoker, we would appreciate your answers to the following questions; they will be kept in strictest confidence.)

1. How many cigarettes per day do you smoke? _____

2. Do any other members of your household smoke? Yes [ ] No [ ]
  If so, how many and what relation are they to you?
  _____

3. How many years have you smoked? _____

4. How many attempts have you made to quit? _____

5. What method(s) have you used in making these attempts?
  _____

6. Do you have any health problems now that are directly caused or aggravated by smoking? Yes [ ] No [ ]
  If so, what are they? _____

7. Have you ever been told to quit smoking by your doctor?   Yes [ ] No [ ]

8. Are you familiar with the company plan to help you quit smoking?   Yes [ ] No [ ]

If "no", would you like materials sent directly to you?   _____

9. Would you (and your smoking dependents) attend an introductory session at your work facility to find out more about the smoking program?   Yes [ ] No [ ]

The following are benefits that you can hope to receive when you quit smoking. Number the items below in the order of their importance to you. Place a zero next to the ones that do not apply to you.)

1. __Get rid of my cough
2. __Set a better example for my children and/or family
3. __Breathe easier
4. __Reduce the risk of serious illness
5. __Improve the quality of my day-to-day life
6. __Feel more in control of my life and my destiny
7. __Have more energy and stamina
8. __Stop throwing money away
9. __Sleep better and wake up more rested

Why You have not quit before now. An American Cancer Society survey of smokers who had thought about quitting identified five major reasons why they were putting it off. If you have found yourself using any of the following reasons in the past, indicate by placing a check next to it.

[ ] 1. The right time had not presented itself.
[ ] 2. Fear of withdrawal discomforts.
[ ] 3. Fear of failure.
[ ] 4. Fear of the unknown because I've been smoking for so many years.
[ ] 5. Feeling that I enjoyed cigarettes even though the overall habit is a liability.

HOW ADDICTED TO CIGARETTES ARE YOU?

Everyone needs to quit smoking since there is no such thing as a safe cigarette or a safe dosage for tar, nicotine or many of the over 200 chemicals found in cigarettes. The test below is designed to measure your degree of physical and psychological addiction. Statistics show that how you score on a quiz like this has nothing to do with whether or not you will actually quit. But we do know that your level of addiction is related to your motivation to take action at any given time. If any of the statements below are true for you right now, check the box on the left.

[ ]   1. Do you, an otherwise polite and considerate person, feel it is your right to smoke whenever and wherever you feel like you need it?

[ ]   2. Do you blame your smoker's cough and sinus trouble on an allergy, a cold, or on everything but the real cause?

[ ]   3. Do you tell yourself you can quit smoking any time you like?

[ ]   4. Do you use as an excuse for not quitting the fact that you'll put on weight?

[ ]   5. Do you feel the need to light up a cigarette everytime someone else does?

[ ]   6. Do you feel betrayed and envious when a fellow smoker quits and tells you how much better he feels?

[ ]   7. Do you try to hide from those close to you the true dimensions of your smoking habit?

[ ]   8. Does your excessive smoking cause trouble between you and loved ones who want you to quit?

[ ]   9. Have you ever run out of cigarettes and borrowed one from a person you didn't know very well--or, worse yet, a total stranger?

[ ] 10. Do you reach for a cigarette when you are socially ill at ease, or uptight?

[ ] 11. Do you have a love-hate relationship with cigarettes?

[ ] 12. Were you reluctant to take this test for fear of how you would do?

If you answered 'yes' to:

9 or more--you will have to work very hard to build your motivation to quit but you can definitely do it!

4 to 8 questions--your motivational level is about average and with the right support you will quit although you won't have the easiest time in the world.

0 to 3 questions--you need only to resolve WHEN and HOW you will quit.

STEPS FOR CREATING A SMOKE-FREE ENVIRONMENT

While every company has unique circumstances that must be considered individually when contemplating a smoke-free environment, we have listed below some of the common steps companies need to make to accomplish this goal.

1.   Examine the Research--Take a close, careful look at the reasons why a nonsmoking environment is desirable for your company. An examination of the cost factors should begin with a talk with your life, disability, industrial accident, health, and fire insurance companies. Your attorneys should be able to provide you with specific information concerning the legal issue for your companies. Ramifications relating to corporate image and social issues need to be aired. Additionally, research concerning productivity is also relevant. A study of these factors should help establish a clear direction for your company concerning the smoking issue. The odds are extremely good that your decision will be to become a smoke-free company.

2. Involve Your Workforce in the Decision-Making--We explained the importance of this earlier. Even if you choose not to establish an employee task force for looking into this issue, a simple employee poll to determine the extent of the employee mandate, is advisable. Employees likely will favor a smoke-free environment by a margin of 3- or 4-to-1. An expanded survey questionnaire circulated to all employees could elucidate a number of the important social and/or legal issues relating to this workplace change.

3. Develop a Comprehensive Plan--this written plan should include a clear statement of the company's intentions and many of the elements described in the steps listed below.

4. Timetable the Transition--in most situations, the time from the announcement of the policy to 100% compliance should be at least 6 months. If your policy is announced August 1 for instance, it might go into effect on February 1 of the following year.

5. Reduce Exposure to Smoke--during the transition period to a total smoke-free environment, limit the areas where smokers can go to have a cigarette. Some will choose this time to quit on their own and others will have a constant reminder of the impending policy if they have to go out of their way every time they choose to light up. Continue to communicate the facts concerning the harmful effects of smoking. The tobacco industry is currently spending millions of dollars on sophisticated advertising dealing with the rights of smokers. They are very concerned about what is happening in the workplace. Countering this publicity also requires a degree of sophistication.

6. Make It Easy and Inexpensive for Employees to Quit During Transition--toward the beginning of the transition period, about the second month, hold the first on-site smoking control program.. A second smoking program is also recommended. (This second one is not announced to the employees, otherwise most all smokers will wait to attend it.) You may feel that one program is enough, but remember, at no time in the smoker's life (with the possible exception of those who are told they must quit by their doctor) will he/she be made more aware of the importance of quitting as during this transition period. These programs should address all aspects of smokers' problems; physical, psychological, and emotional.

7. Make the Official Day of Enactment a Special Day--for the employees who will understand that the policy is important and it will be enforced. Many companies have used this time promote favorable publicity.

INCENTIVES THAT ENHANCE PARTICIPATION, AND FOLLOW-THROUGH

Estimates of the annual cost to employ a smoker go as high as $5,000 per year. While many different methods work for paying the stop-smoking program fee, the company should be prepared to provide incentives to smokers who quit and remain abstinent. Money should not be a reason for any smoker not to participate in these clinics. The company should be prepared use payroll deductions if necessary. One health promotion manager was looking for a way to increase participation in the "Great American Smokeout," a national media event sponsored by the American Lung Association to bring attention to the health hazards of smoking by promoting one day of smoking cessation. She decided to hold a raffle whose participants were only those who quit smoking for one day. Each smoker who stopped for the entire day got one chance at the prize. And what was the prize? A cold turkey, of course! Actually, it was frozen. Participation was greatly increased over the previous year.

There was no doubt in this organizer's mind that this reward, although modest, increased participation while adding humor and tangible value to the promoted event. Are incentives and rewards always this easy? Not always, but this example does help us understand that even small rewards that cost little or no money can have dramatic impact. Here are a few other examples of some general categories of incentives that might enhance your workplace health promotion events:

> **Belonging**--Everyone likes to feel a part of something which can be enhanced
> by using T-shirts, certificates, and membership cards.
> **Recognition**--This need can be reinforcedby newsletter
> recognition, trophies, award ceremonies, wall charts, etc.
> **Special Privilege**--This has been done through such things as employee parking and
> healthy employee days.
> **Games**--This could include drawings and raffles as well as using lottery tickets as prizes.
> This may not always seen as a positive value.

Time reward--This involves participation on company time or even a special paid day off work.

Money--This could include everything from cash awards to reimbursements of fees spent to quit smoking.

Competition/challenge--More and more program organizers are using the natural competitiveness of the workplace to motivate employees to change lifestyle habits. Some of these were discussed earlier in this chapter.

Workplace incentives come down to finding the right motivational tools for your particular employees. When you find and use them effectively, you can expect increased participation and follow through, and a more successful program.

FACTORS AGAINST WORKPLACE HP INCENTIVES

In spite of having top management support,having a well planned HP program and using incentives, you might find a participation rate less than expected. If this occurs look at the organizational factors that may be undermining success. Once identified, you may be able to turn a negative factor into a positive one.

1. **Certain company policies**--These may include liberal sick leave policies as well as a workplace with no smoking restrictions.

2. **Management style**--These could be those where an adversarial relation exists between management and labor, as well as ones characterized by general aloofness.

3. **Structure of health care benefits packages**--If employees have "first dollar coverage, they may lack incentive to contain health costs.

4. **Workplace health norms**--This may include going to the popular "watering hole" after work.

5. **Physical environment**--An unsafe environment with a history of safety violations.

QUALITY CONTROL CHECKLIST

Success of the overall effort is often dependent on how discriminating you are when choosing or developing an HP programs. You can have the best plan, understand the organizational needs, and market effectively; but if you do not have effective programs, the effort is for naught. The following checklist is designed to help the manager, administrator, or coordinator ask the right questions and address the relevant issues.

[ ]   **1.**   Check credentials and/or references of presenters.
[ ]   **2.**   Will presentation style be effective for our workforce?
[ ]   **3.**   Is the goal for this program clearly stated to presenter?
[ ]   **4.**   What handouts and written materials will be used?
[ ]   **5.**   Will these written materials provide participant with framework for individualized follow-up?
[ ]   **6.**   Is presenter's philosophy/attitude/presentation consistent with program's goals?
[ ]   **7.**   What provisions are made for cultural support of activity?
[ ]   **8.**   What workplace incentives and reward sdoes presenter recommend?
[ ]   **9.**   How has presenter measured success rate in the past, and what measures are proposed for this program?
[ ] **10.**   What is the cost of implementing this program and what are the potential benefits?

7

EVALUATION FOR BOTTOM-LINE RESULTS

INTRODUCTION

Evaluation of human resource activities of any kind within organizational settings is one of the least understood areas of the whole field of HR development. The task of evaluating health promotion activities is even newer and less understood. It recalls the story of the pilot who spoke to his passengers over the airplane intercom system in mid-flight, "Ladies and gentlemen, good afternoon. This is your captain speaking. I have two announcements to make--one good and one bad. First the good one; we are making excellent time! Now the bad news; we are lost!"

We do vast amounts of training, education, and development in human resources including, in recent years, health promotion programs. Yet do we know how effective our programs really are? The issue of accountability relates to a very basic question asked by all responsible organizations: What have you done with the resources we have given you? The easy answer is the one we have most often given and involves the quantitative aspects of evaluations. For health promotion programs, this means the informal process of evaluation; i.e., number of programs offered, number of participants. This is an important part of the evaluative process, but in most instances not as revealing as the qualitative issues.

This chapter will define and briefly describe some of the important terms used in the evaluation of health promotion programs. It will also summarize some of the important issues of HP evaluation. It is not our intention to provide readers with an extensive methodological discussion.

Too often evaluation of programs, products, and services is given only casual attention. Even though the evaluation comes after the planning, assessment, and implementation stages, decisions about what is to be evaluated, who will be doing the evaluation, the manner in which the evaluation is to occur, and, finally, the uses for information obtained in the evaluation process need to be made from the beginning--prior to the assessment and implementation stages.

The measurement and evaluation of program outcomes has become the single most important activity in the still young field of health promotion, according to *Opatz, 1986.* Early organizational supporters of health promotion programs were personally committed to encouraging wellness programs because they made sense, but the time for blind acceptance of health promotion efficacy has passed. Some programs that had foregone evaluation of their programs in favor of investing those dollars in program activities are in deep trouble. Corporate executives are now wanting data that supports the justification of programs. Health promotion program planners are responding by establishing programs with clear expectations and measurable outcomes.

There are some health promotion managers and professionals who have the necessary skills to perform an effective, credible evaluation of their programs; however, most health promotion professionals come from health-related fields that include neither the financial/management skills nor the measurement expertise needed for comprehensive program evaluation. This chapter addresses a number of issues that will help to understand and meet the new challenge for program accountability.

KEY TERMS USED IN HP EVALUATION

Moberg (1984), defines HP evaluation as: "The systematic collection, analysis and interpretation of data for the purpose of determining the value of a social policy or program, to be used in decision-making about the program."

There are three key aspects to this definition: **First,** data collection is systematic; it is planned in advance and follows specific procedures for sampling, documentation, verification, and validation. **Second,** the value or merit of a program must be determined, either relative to other alternative activities, or to a set of goals or criteria of success. **Third,** the purpose of evaluation sets it apart from other forms of research because evaluation is used to make decisions about the program.

USES OF EVALUATION

How can we use the data (information) we collect to evaluate our health promotion programs? Some purposes are listed below.

1. Accountability. This is the most common, and many believe most important use of evaluation at all program levels.
2. Program planning and development.
3. To help program personnel systematically examine what they are doing and why.
4. To assist in program improvement.
5. Dissemination of program models i.e., sharing information regarding positive outcomes.

FORMATIVE EVALUATIONS

The Formative Evaluation is the continuous and informal process of reassessing and improving ongoing program activities. Most health promotion planners collect information for this purpose, including:

1. Number of programs offered.
2. Number of participants
3. Selection of program topics
4. Feedback from group leaders and instructors
5. Opinions and feedback of participants

The following is an example of an opinion and feedback evaluation form:

PARTICIPANT EVALUATION FORM

Company Name: _____

Program Name: _____ Date: _____

Instructor' Name: _____

Please circle the number that is appropriate for each question:

1. How satisfied were you with this program?

          1   2   3   4   5

    Very unsatisfied   Very satisfied

    Comment: _____

2. Will you be able to use the information presented in this program to help you make positive changes in your lifestyle?

          1   2   3   4   5

    It won't help me   It will help me

    Comment: _____

3. How much improvement would you recommend in the program content, materials, presentation, time, length, etc?

          1   2   3   4   5

    Many improvements   No improvements

    Comment: _____

    _____

    _____

We thank you for your time and input!

SUMMATIVE EVALUATION

This is the more importanttype of evaluation. It is a more formal process that is the systematic preplanned effort to obtain data and information used to determine the effectiveness of completed programs. There are two primary targets for summative evaluation.

The **first** is the assessment of specific program results to determine if they have achieved their intended objectives. For example: Your company has offered an on-site weight program to all their employees. Upper management has agreed to reimburse the total program fee to each participant who loses x% of their starting body weight (prescreening is required) and keeps it off for a period of six months. You have determined that the program should have the following objective: 50% of the participants achieve "significant" weight loss and maintain it for a period of six months. Your first task is to collect the data that determines whether or not this has been achieved.

The **second** role of summative evaluation is to determine the appropriateness of the goals and objectives of the program. Using the same example, your second task is to determine the appropriateness of the goal. Is the goal of weight reduction important? Is a 50% success rate appropriate? How, or to what degree, did this program component contribute to the overall success of the health promotion effort? What is the cost incurred by the organization for this component relative to the benefit received? This is the cost-benefit ratio.

HP Goals Amenable to Summative Evaluation Measures

Good health promotion programs will probably have one or more of the following goals. The first four relate to individual measures and each can be seen as a level of goal that requires slightly greater evaluative sophistication than the one preceding it. The final three goals reflect the need for HP facilitators to demonstrate a positive program impact on the organization.

1. Increased knowledge about health and lifestyle factors that affect health. This is one the earliest summative measures we can evaluate. Since increased knowledge of health issues is positively correlated with healthy lifestyles, inferences can be made based on some measurable aspect of this increase. As mentioned previously, some of the most common organizational health promotion components come under the heading of knowledge acquisition due to organizational constraints on time, money, and person power. Following the lead established by many companies for occupational health and safety programs, some health promotion facilitators are beginning to use pen and pencil quizzes and interactive video to obtain feedback related to knowledge retention. Linking these activities to competitions and rewards can help maintain and increase participation.

2. Changes in health-related behaviors. Most program facilitators will want to measure changes in personal health habits as a result of their HP program. These health habits may influence such workplace behavior as emotional well-being, job satisfaction, alcohol and drug abuse, or management of work-related stress. What percent of your workforce smokes now versus before you implemented a smoke-free workplace policy or provided a smoking cessation program? What percent of those employees who achieved significant weight loss through a workplace program have maintained their weight loss at six months? These questions should be asked and the appropriate records kept.

3. Reduction in risk factors. Positive changes in lifestyle habits often affect one or more risks factors. One of the easiest and most cost-effective ways to measure this is through the administration of a before and after Health Risk Appraisal (HRA). Even with its limitations, an HRA, such as the one researched and distributed by the *Center for Disease Control,* can provide useful data regarding changes in the major risk factors.

4. Reduction in early death and disease. Since a reduction in early death and disease is the inferred reason for having the three previous personal wellness goals, this is frequently a long-term objective of most comprehensive health promotion programs. The HRA is one way to measure this.

5. Reduction in absenteeism. Most HP evaluations target absenteeism since it is both a visible and costly workplace indicator of individual health. To evaluate this effectively, the HP evaluator needs access to personnel records in order to control for such things as The Healthy Worker Effect, since many wellness program participants are usually among the healthiest in any organizational setting.

6. Reduction in health care and other benefit costs. For many health promotion programs,reducing costs is one of the core objectives.Collecting data for evaluation requires access to personal medical records and can be a labor-intensive evaluative activity. It is also important to remember that cost reduction is a long-term goal.

7. Enhanced public image. In recent years, many companies began health promotion programs because they seemed like the right public relations thing to do. Some of the larger Fortune 500 companies have gotten a lot of PR exposure out of their high-visibility programs. Some programs were designed and implemented with much thought and planning while others were not. Questions have been raised concerning some of the published results of these programs because many companies were too quick to declare huge savings from these efforts, but there is no doubt about the public relations value of HP programs.

LEVELS OF EVALUATION
The following three levels of evaluation are usually not implemented all at the same time in the evaluation effort. These levels are included to provide you

with a sense of the range of possibilities in the evaluation process. As *Moberg (1984)* explains, "evaluation is not a single method, design, or approach, but a smorgasbord from which to pick and choose as appropriate to accountability requirement, your information needs, and the available resources."

The Process Level: The inputs and activities of the program itself are useful for formative evaluation, for describing staff and participant characteristics, interactions, and transactions; for understanding the program's theory; for needs assessment; and for detailed description and documentation of the services actually rendered. Process data is useful both in day-to-day management and planning activitiesor in disseminating a program model for possible implementation or replication at another site. Process evaluation often focuses on effort, regardless of output or effectiveness. The data is the same as formative evaluation: How many employees actually enrolled in the smoking cessation program? How does the number of enrollees relate to the number who originally said they wanted to attend? How many enrollees liked the program?

Outcome Evaluation: This level examines the attainment of program objectives related to short- and long-term change in participants' behavior, attitudes, or knowledge. Attaining satisfactory outcomes is the primary or reason that programs are established, and thus it deserves attention in most program evaluation efforts. For example: The smoking cessation program would have a successful outcome if a meaningful percentage of participants did not begin to smoke in the near future. Efficiency may also be examined and measured as part of an outcome study. Efficiency involves the consideration of alternative strategies for minimizing costs while maximizing outcomes. Could the same outcome level be accomplished at less cost in terms of money, time, personnel, participant time, energy, and inconvenience? Cost-benefit and cost-effectiveness research measure program efficiency. What is the ratio of monetary return the organization can expect as a result of the smoking cessation program? Is it cost effective to conduct this program on-site?

Impact Evaluation: This level refers to the assessment of longer-term, generalized results of program operation and relates to the organizational needs and problems which led to the establishment of the program. Impact evaluation helps to ascertain whether the total effect of the program has been beneficial. The key difference between outcome and impact evaluation is that outcome considers only the direct program participants, while impact is concerned with the target population. For example, has the outcome of this program helped to further the organizational objectives? Has it provided a smoke-free work environment foremployees, and reduced organizational health care costs?

Additional Considerations

The task of program evaluation can be difficult for those inexperienced in instrument design and statistical analysis. Many health promotion coordinators will find it useful to seek the advise and/or involvement of experts in this area to complete complex evaluation studies. The following are often used as guidelines by competent researchers when conducting these studies:

Clarity--Is the purpose clearly understood and articulated prior to the onset of the evaluation process? Having unambiguously phrased hypotheses should provide this clarity.

Validity--Does the study evaluate what was intended? If the effect of a fitness program on health care resource utilization patterns are being measured, are there control mechanisms for the fact that the healthiest employees are the most likely to enroll?

Reliability--Do the measurements used provide accurate information? For instance, how reliable is the Center for Disease Control Health Risk Appraisal in predicting risk factors for early death and disease?

Objectivity--Are the interpretations of the findings consistent among multiple observers? The organizational environment (particularly corporate) is not the ideal research setting. Often biases and conflict with other corporate objectives will displace objective interpretations.

Need--Does the scope of the evaluation meet its intended need? Is it over- or under-designed? A study to determine the effect of a smoking cessation program on health costs over time would be under-designed if you had to rely on only the responses of individual participants to provide data on health care utilization. Access to the health claims records is needed to confirm results.

Credibility--Will the outcomes of the evaluation be used in making program decisions? This is partly a people issue. Often, due to organizational politics or other considerations, program changes indicated by the the evaluation will not be possible to implement, or at least within an optimum time frame.

EVALUATION PLANNING STEPS

We have previously stressed that performing an evaluation is not a simple matter of applying a set of predetermined techniques. Rather, the evaluation must be developed and tailored to the unique circumstances of the program under scrutiny. Of prime concern is the usefulness of the evaluation to the key decision-makers and others who are involved. The following is an overview of the steps recommended by researchers in planning and carrying out program evaluations. It is recommended that the individual or group who is actively involved in the evaluation implementation, reports findings directly to the HP program task force or planning committee. This will support the key issue of "ownership" of the program. We will again use the example of the smoking cessation program as a model.

Step #1: Identify and organize relevant information users and key decision makers. Your development of an evaluation strategy should always involve the evaluator and key staff. In most organizational settings the evaluator will be a designated staff member or administrator. Potential members of this group of decision-makers should be people who:

1. Want and can use the information.
2. Have questions they want answered.
3. Will be able to act on the basis of evaluation information.d
4. Will be willing to devote time to and share responsibility for the evaluation.

Step #2: Identify and refine the relevant evaluation questions. The evaluation group must first determine the broad purposes of the evaluation and choose from among the many alternatives available. They need to address these key questions: Is the evaluation to be formative or summative? Should it emphasize process, outcome, or impact issues? What data will be required to conduct an effective evaluation and how will it be conducted?

The evaluation will be both formative and summative since we want to know such issues as how many attended, how the enrollees perceived the program, how many quit initially and remained quit, and how this benefited the organization. Process, outcome, and impact issues will be emphasized. The evaluation team (or individual) must plan enough time to do the necessary tracking that will provide an adequate evaluation. This includes sending individual feedback forms to participants at three months intervals during the first year and having confidential access to health claims records for all participants, which is necessary in order to show a reduction in utilization in health care resources for this group in the next several years.

Step # 3: Specify goals and objectives. Write down general program goals:

"To provide the means for as many employees as possible to quit smoking in the next year."

Then identify and select the best indicators of goal achievement. Be specific in the level of the achievements:

"Our goal is a 10% reduction in the smoking population."

Translate the indicators into measurable objectives that contain a statement of the indicator and target population, a time frame, and either a statement of the proportion of the target population expected to show change or the amount of change expected on the indicator. This statement format could be:

"_____, _____of _____will _____."
  (By When)   (% Change)   (Who)   (What)

The written version might look like this:

"By 12/31/88, 10% of the smoking population of our company will have quit smoking and remained quit for a period of six (or 12) months."

Step#4: Select evaluation methods appropriate to the evaluation questions. Having determined the focal evaluation questions and the program's goals and objectives, select a method of obtaining the necessary data to answer the questions posed. While some approaches specifically require the collection of new data, others can use existing information or simply review the program as described in existing documentation. Although there may be others, evaluation questions include the following:

Prestructured or allowed to vary with accumulating data? (Fixed or Dynamic) Since we are dealing with a life-style habit/addiction that requires total abstinence in order for success to be achieved, the data collection process is easier when compared to other habit management programs, i.e., stress management. A prestructured (fixed) method is preferred. What percent of program participants quit initially? How many remained abstinent at three, six, and twelve months? How does our outcome impact the organization?

Concern with past participants or future participants? (Prospective or retrospective) If a smoking cessation program has been previously conducted in this organizational setting, many inferences can be made based on a retrospective analysis of the data collected. However, our focus will be on the prospective participants.

Focus on total program or on specific parts? (Holistic or Component) This is one aspect of a larger program and is therefore a component focus.

Test specific hypotheses about the program, or develop generalizations based on the data? (Deductive or Inductive) Continuing the example previously given, our hypotheses concerning the program will be:

1. *Ten percent of the smoking population of our organization will quit smoking and remain abstinent in the next twelve months.*

2. *As a result of hypothesis #1, this reduction will result in a savings of X dollars in health care costs over the next three years, due to decreased utilization of health care resources.*

Compare groups receiving the program to similar groups who do not, or look only at program participants? (Between-group or within-group analysis.) We would probably choose to do both since the organization is actively promoting nonsmoking behavior. Some motivated smokers will choose to quit on their own and could serve as a control group. We will also want to measure success rates for individual participants.

Step #5:Develop an evaluation implementation strategy. The evaluation plan will likely include:

A. A statement of the evaluation questions(s)
B. A description of the evaluation method: The data being collected, from whom, and using what techniques.
C. Who will be responsible for each evaluation task.

D. Plans for summarization and analysis.
E. Time lines for all phases of the evaluation, including data collection, analysis, and reporting.
F. Plans for use of the information.

Step #6: Implement the evaluation plan. It is important that the person responsible for the evaluation monitors all aspects because there are many areas where procedures that have serious potential for harming the evaluation can breakdown. Some potential problem areas include the following:

A. Failure to record and collect the data.
B. Reconstruction of data long after-the-fact, with inherent inaccuracies.
C. Breakdown of confidentiality protection procedures.
D. Biased sampling, particularly of program recipients.

Step #7: Summarize, analyze, and interpret the data. Depending upon the approach used, data summarization, analysis, and interpretation will either be an on- going process which occurs simultaneously with data collection or will be a separate step which occurs after all data have been collected.

OTHER KEY ISSUES IN EVALUATION

Over the past decade employers' health care costs have increased at a rate of about 16% per year. Employers spent $97.2 billion on health care in 1984 compared with $25.5 billion in 1975. As employers have become increasingly aware of their rising health care expenditures and consequent diversion of funds from other employee benefits and corporate missions, they have implemented a variety of strategies in an attempt to more effectively manage these costs.

Workplace health promotion is just one strategy in cost management effort. As with other programs ,these programs can have costs without effects, but they cannot have effects without costs. Therefore, increasing numbers of health promotion directors are being required to discuss with corporate decision makers not only who they are and what they do, but how much they cost the organization. This circumstance has produced a heightened interest among program evaluators in various cost evaluative techniques.

The above techniques have ranged from purely descriptive procedures, such as cost analysis and cost outcome analysis, to those permitting direct comparison of program costs to program benefits, such as cost-benefit analysis. Although the number of cost evaluation procedures is quite large, the two which have received the most attention among health care professionals are cost-benefit analysis and cost-effectiveness analysis. Both procedures will probably become more prevalent in the years to come, so it is very important that their correct use, as well as their limitations are well understood.

Cost-benefit analysis usually involves identifying the dollar value required to achieve program objectives and the dollar value resulting from achievement of those objectives. One of the most common methods for comparing costs and benefits involves subtracting the dollar value of the benefits from the dollar value of the costs, thus enabling the evaluator to determine whether the program has resulted in a net gain or a net loss. The other most commonly used method for comparing costs and benefits is the cost-benefit ratio which is calculated by dividing all program related benefits by all program costs. A health promotion planner might calculate the cost-benefit ratio for a smoking cessation program by using the following numbers (These are hypothetical, but they reflect best estimates based on the authors' experience):

STATISTICAL SUMMARY OF
SMOKING CESSATION PROGRAM RESULTS

Employee Data

1,000	Employees
280	Smoked at the beginning of the program
50	Express strong desire to quit
30	Completed the program and are nonsmokers
18	Remained abstinent for one year
6	Quit on own and remained quit for one year.
24	Total abstainers after one year

Summary of Program Cost Per Enrollee

$275	Program fee per enrollee
125	Administrative costs per enrollee
$400	Total cost per enrollee

Reimbursement Policy

One-half of program fee reimbursed after 6 months, and remaining half reimbursed at end of year if employee quits and remains abstinent for one year. Those who return to smoking after 6 months, but before one-year receive the first reimbursement only.

Year One Program Costs (Incurred by Company)

$ 2,475 Full Cost Paid by Unsuccessful Enrollees (9 X $275)
___411 One-half Cost Paid by Those Who Smoked After 6 Mos. (3 X $137)
$ 2,886 Total Employee Paid Cost

$12,000 Company Cost For 30 enrollees at $400 each
_-2,886 Less Employee Paid Cost
<$ 9,114> Total program cost for first year

Year One Monetary Benefits

For the combined categories of reduced absenteeism and fewer medical claims, a documented, highly conservative cost savings of $625 per successful employee was recorded.The reasons for this conservative savings is that during the first year of quitting, positive health changes come slowly.

$15,000 = Total monetary benefit in year one of smoking program
($625 X 24 = $15,000)

Cost-Benefit Ratio For Year One
<$9,114> = Cost+ $15,000 = Benefit, then
Cost-Benefit Ratio = 9,114/15,000 = 1: 6.076

This ratio means that for every one dollar invested in the program (cost), a return of $6.08 was recorded (benefit). Starting with year two, the cost-benefit ratio should be even more favorable since program costs would be confined to data collection, analysis, and interpretation.

A cost-benefit analysis can be applied to a program during its planning stage or after it has been in operation. The major difference between the two approaches is that the former requires many more assumptions and cost estimates than does the latter. Since there are empirical data on actual costs and benefits in a post cost-benefit analysis, its results are usually far more accurate and reliable. For an evaluator, the easiest part of a cost-benefit analysis involves determining the direct costs of a program. In a retrospective analysis, there is usually a record of actual expenditures while in a prospective analysis there is a proposed budget for the program.

Cost-Effective Analysis is an alternative approach to cost evaluation that does not require monetizing benefits. This approach compares program costs measured in dollars--to program effects--measured in whatever units are appropriate. This procedure permits the ranking of various program alternatives according to the size of their effect relative to their costs. However, since costs and effects are in different units, it does not permit direct comparison of program costs to benefits. Although it is possible to conduct these analyses prospectively, virtually all analyses are retrospective.

These prospective cost-effective analyses are typically less accurate and less reliable than the retrospective ones. As with cost-benefit analysis, there are also limitations to the use of cost-effectiveness approaches to cost evaluation. One obvious shortcoming results from an analysis that does not lead to any clear-cut decision. This occurs when comparing two program alternatives where one is either less or more costly and effective than the other. This problem can occasionally be solved using efficiency criteria, such as choosing on the basis of the amount of effect per-unit-of-cost.

Cost-Benefit Versus Cost Effectiveness Analyses
Cost-benefit analysis and cost effectiveness analysis are not interchangeable procedures. Cost-benefit analysis is most useful for evaluating a single program while cost-effectiveness analysis is most useful for selecting the most efficient program from among various alternatives. Although cost-benefit and cost-effectiveness analyses are different and are usually used in different circumstances, the basic steps involved in each are essentially the same. Here we will summarize:

1. Define exactly what comprises the programs and examine the services, clientele, and operating conditions of the program.
2. Determine the possible direct (tangible, i.e., reduced absenteeism) and indirect (intangible, i.e., improved employee-employer relationship) impacts of the program.
3. Establish one or more measures of each impact.
4. Identify those impacts which should be measured and measure them. Monetize the impacts of cost-benefit analysis.
5. Establish an investigative design which will have internal and external validity in estimating the net impact of the program.
6. Determine the operating costs of the program.
7. Disseminate the results and discuss them with the appropriate audiences, emphasizing how the results relate to the investigative methodology and the assumptions made in the estimation process.

All of these steps are important; however, the ultimate justification of either analysis rests on the assumption that the results will improve decision making.

8

EFFECTIVE MARKETING STRATEGIES

INTRODUCTION

The assessment of needs and development of a good HP program is not enough to ensure an effective program. Promoting and marketing helps management and employees become better aware of the unique features of your program. Promotion must reflect what both leadership and employees want in an HP program and what they are willing to support,it then tries to match the expectations and commitments of both groups. Promoters of programs must challengethe attitudes of those not yet convinced of the benefits of a healthier lifestyle as well as providing for the needs of those who are presently involved in wellness. If marketing/promoting efforts are only limited to present buyers or consumers, thereby "saving the saved," while offering wonderful benefits to those already pursuing a healthy lifestyle, your efforts will have little impact on the larger population to whom the programs must be directed, and on whom achievement of long-term objectives depend.

HP Promotion Definition: A set of planned strategies undertaken by health promotion consultants, managers, or planners to first, win approval from top management (decision makers), then to develop, implement, and constantly evaluate the proper match of products and services with the needs of the organizational client or consumer, in order to facilitate HP and organizational system goals. Marketing/promoting is the process that transfers the product or service to the end user, who in the case of health promotion, may be a client company or an employee group.

Good promotion of programs helps customers/employees become aware of and establish some value for your service. Internal marketing HP services requires that you become very familiar with your prospective customer(s) and their company vision, mission, goals and objectives. The following are examples of HP program goals

1. Increased productivity.
2. Improved morale.
3. Reduced health care/insurance costs.
4. Improved image.
5. Improved Human Resource Management/Development (reduced absenteeism, turnover, training costs).
6. Fewer health claims.
7. Better work culture/climate.
8. Reduced work stress.

Not only do organizations want these things, but they must be willing to invest money and resources to achieve them. It is also important to consider the needs, motivations, goals and objectives of individuals:

1. Need help to change poor health habits/behavior.
2. Improve personal goal attainment and self-esteem through planning.
3. Want to be more attractive.
4. Desire to have more energy.
5. Need to have something left of themselves after work.
6. Want their families to get along better.

The goals of marketing and of health promotion are not necessarily incompatible. We believe that marketing is important to consider in the planning and design of your HP system, policies, and programs. If you have followed the general philosophy of this book, i.e., open systems and OD concepts, you will understand the commitment we feel toward building a productive and dignified community of workers. Our non-manipulative approach still requires the firm belief that in order to create a productive workplace we must care about the needs of our workers. If HP can assist in this task, then use the most effective marketing methods possible. Non-profit health and educational foundations use good marketing strategies and plans and even charities organize conferences on the techniques of marketing. Ethically sensitive and socially conscious marketing is essential to a long-term successful outcome.

Marketing is working toward the formulation and delivery of effective programs. The development and implementation of solid programs requires communication, assessing response and feedback patterns, resources, support, participation and wide sponsorship. It is just not a good marketing strategy to say, "We have this HP program and we are going to get people to participate in it whether they like it or not." Our goals should be to foster the values of general health awareness, productive system development, wide-participation, and increased quality of life--including productive work, both personally and organizationally. However, we must still think of effectively involving our client-employees and they must "buy" (participate) this service to achieve our mutual benefits.

Promotion and marketing is not restricted to advertising and public relations, but is one aspect. But even more, promotion concerns how we communicate our program's mission, goals, and benefits with good ethics and honesty. Promotion should allow us to reach our target audiences with our message. Of course, we want them to purchase (participate) our product (service) because we believe in it, and know that it meets real needs/interest determined through our research and assessments. Needs assessments, interest surveys, and marketing research are not so very different. For example, a needs assessment can focus on health needs by utilizing an HRA (Health Risk Appraisal) or some other health assessment. Market research may expand on this and may not only address physiological needs, but psychological and social needs as well. What do you think you need? How shall we package it? What channels of communication can we use to talk to you? Where is the best place to deliver our message? Needs assessments should be expanded to include such consumer perceptions.

SERVICE PROMOTION/MARKETING
When we talk about buyer or consumers in the service arena, we must change our perspective regarding how clients value what we provide. In fact, we are actually talking about how employees and employers within any organization will respond to our health promotion/wellness message. Does our health promotion program appeal to specific groups' needs and wants? There are limits to mass market appeals. Can we convert their emerging interests, needs or desires into participation, and eventual behavior change? Will the HP program be continuously and loyally supported, and will it be adequately funded over a reasonable period of time? These questions

become more difficult to answer since we are marketing an intangible service versus a tangible product. When clients/employees buy our service they are only buying the promise that we will deliver what we have promised to deliver. They may be more unsure of what we are actually offering, and whether it is being presented at a reasonable price in terms of lost work time, incentive or even cost to the organization. The challenge is to find more concrete ways to make our promise tangible, more similar to a product that has concrete benefits.

Being sensitive to the above needs, demands that our approach should be informational, with a distinctly soft-sell emphasis. This means avoiding the temptation to start the HP program for the wrong reasons. We certainly do not want to start off our promotional efforts by giving the perception that HP is a top-management ploy to create information than can used to our disadvantage or an invasion of privacy.

The need for an upbeat, positive, supportive emphasis demands that we take a participative, system-wide and sensitive posture. How do we define and assess benefits, measure and evaluate results, and reinforce or build loyalty and support for our HP service product in a way that supports the quality and effectiveness of the HP program entire organizational system? We can only do this through effective planning and development strategies that include responsive promotional and marketing techniques. These techniques involve basic human relations skills--listening, communicating, participating and monitoring in a highly sensitive and responsive manner. It is a difficult, but highly rewarding opportunity for health promotion professionals, particularly, if they know the needs, characteristics, values, wants, and life-style preferences of their employee/clients. Often people do not think about preventive maintenance of their health until they are sick and need to see the doctor. They may know they are not living or working well, but have no sense of urgency to do anything about it. As we have discussed earlier, many workers only have a vague idea of the definition of health promotion or wellness. Their knowledge stops with the need for better weight control, exercise and diet. How can we convince these employees to think about prevention, and the link between life-style behavior and health consequences, if they do not know that prevention reduces their long-term health risks? How do we personalize this linkage and increase its importance, when the impacts occur over long periods of years, and we are competing with each other for more time and space to explore our own expressive needs? *(Yankelovich, 1981)* The answer is that we need to think very carefully about tactics and strategies for reaching our target markets. Promotion can help publicize the reasons/rationale behind our program, in addition to listing the activities and describing offered programs. Marketing/promotion can also help with program development and implementation since publicity and participatory activities help future participants understand the generic link between good health behavior and a more effective and productive life.

Marketing is not focused on specific actions that each person should do, but conveys the message about personally responsible health behavior and actions. Thus, as promoters we must identify existing client needs and resources, matching our products and services with our clients' existing information. In this way we can determine which health behavior needs are important or cause discomfort. We need to also understand how to provide more relevant and meaningful information, skills, information and behaviors to improve our employees' work efforts.

Promotion/marketing begins with a plan for assessing the needs of our target groups, and with identifying factors that may impede or promote acceptance of our services and programs. We then identify, design and implement issues such as the strategies that will effectively sell and deliver what we provide. Finally, we must plan the monitoring and evaluation of our system that will measure its effectiveness. We can view marketing as an integral adjunct to program planning and development. As we have stated throughout this book, our success will be determined by how well we match company objectives/programs with employees' views, values, feelings, thoughts, needs and interests. The organizational needs analysis can function as an adjunct to, or as the sole basis of the promotional plan. It helps us acquire the big view of the organization that targets potential needs and problems, and makes us aware of important potential sponsors, supporters, role models and power brokers. By knowing more about the organization (systems, structures, processes, behavior and its state of health or functioning, we gain a better perspective about how to position our services/products to build interest and serve the real needs of our clients.

GENERIC PROMOTION/MARKETING STRATEGIES

Rapp and Collins (1987) refer to "Maxi-Marketing" which includes a systematic framework and useful ideas regarding promotion and marketing efforts which we have expanded and slightly altered for use in promoting health programs:

1. **Maximized Targeting**--Prospect your clients/supporters and chart the best prospects, while mobilizing those with potential interest. We need specialized and segmented data, information about needs, values, interests, concerns and life-patterns.

2. **Maximized Media**--Make use of opportunities for creating communication linkages and ways to get the word out, building communication links and support networks.

3. **Maximized Accountability**--Provide that it works in the real world by showing results, costs savings and relevance to other management concerns.

4. **Maximized Awareness Advertising**--Appeal to the whole brain through a wide variety of techniques, like creative titles of classes (Safeway calls its running program as "Buns on the Run") new ways of encouraging attendance at health fairs through coupons for free health snack food in the company cafeteria.

5. **Maximized Activation**--Use more Inquiry and dialogue advertising (again, get responses/feedback to discover the degree of interest and awareness).

6. **Maximized Synergy**--Let ads, open houses, health promos do more than one job. Piggyback your information in a company newsletter; put a message in the pay envelopes, or a use special logo or program stamp across company correspondence.

7. **Maximized Linkage**--Encourage interested prospects in new ways; link to past successes, sales, and need patterns; link with other programs in your area for joint activities.

8. **Maximized Sales**--through custom data bases (demographics, needs, life-style preferences, value trends, career dynamics). *Levitt (1986)* states: "What it increasingly takes to make and keep that sale is to tangibilize the intangible, to re state the benefit and its source to the customer/client." Sponsor all employee contests with tangible rewards and prizes.

9. **Maximized Distribution**--Use multiple channels of communication, information, analysis and service to reach the client employee. Also, link to all other mediums of publicity such as union newsletters, bulletin boards, electronic mail, company corre spondence/ paper, general newsletters, quarterly benefits statement).

SEGMENTING AND TARGETING

"If we try to be all things to all people, we wind up being nothing to nobody." Segmentation is taking a look at our target population and saying, "how can we break up that group so that we can have subgroups that have similar needs, characteristics, values, interests, job demands, work environments, leisure interests, professional identification, and committee memberships." We need to break the population down several ways into target market segments.

Demographic Segmentation--Your promotion/marketing effort should take into account the basic statistical categories. For instance, If your workforce is predominantly male and over forty, you probably would not want to plan an aerobic dance class. Below we have listed a few demographic segmentations and then provided some examples. For all of the segmentation categories below, try to think of any additional examples howthat particular segmentation could affect a workplace health promotion program. Can these assumptions be varied? One must be careful that beliefs about certain demographic areas are not based on prejudice but facts.

1. **Young--**Would probably want a different type of exercise program.

2. **Close to retirement age--**risk for heart disease is greater for this group.

3. **Sex--**women in workforce may be more likely to want a weight program, wh ile men may be more interested in exercise or stress reduction.

4. **Marital status--**people are staying single longer, wanting to stay physically attractive, so singles may be more likely to enroll in fitness program.

5. **Income level--**May be able to afford, and more likely to participate in a fee-based programs.

6. **Educational level--**Education is often equated with higher awareness of health issues and more likely to participate.

7. **National origin and race--**Different nationalities and races have different risk factors.

8. **Geographic difference--**A branch of the same company may be located in a much colder climate, thus limiting the time they can spend outdoors doing exercise.

Psychographic Segmentation--Based on the way we feel about ourselves and others, we will be more or less receptive to health promotion. Psychographics include:

1. **Attitudes**--Many people have become disillusioned with the present health care system.

2. **Lifestyles**--This has produced a movement (Megatrend) toward self-care.

3. **Values**--People's value of healthy lifestyle practices vary from place to place and from time to time.

Benefits Segmentation--What benefits do we think we can get from health promotion? Differently perceived benefits from participating in programs or being healthy can motivate people in different ways. Information we glean concerning this dimension will tell us not only what to have in our program, but how to package and market it.

1. **Being or staying skinny**--This may be the benefit that motivates people to enroll in a weight control program.

2. **Being "high fashion"**--These last two segmentations may indicate that to reach these individuals, we may have to market our program like soap.

3. **Peace of mind**--"I won't have to worry if I don't smoke."

Usage Segmentation--Much can be learned about what people will or will not purchase by knowing their buying habits and their preferences for certain consumer goods, services, and programs which may be related to their beliefs and values regarding your product or service. For instance:

1. **A health club member**--More likely to attend wellness program.

2. **A reader of health magazines**--May be interested in self-directed events.

3. **TV dinners and fast food buyers**--May need, but also might be resistant to a nutritional program.

When engaged in service promotion/marketing for HP, the target group's (identified employees') characteristics are very important. Before and during our promotion efforts we need to know as much as possible about our worker population and their attitudes/ beliefs, health habits and behaviors, interests and work subcultures or environments. In order to design and market programs that encourage positive health behaviors, you must understand the negative health attitudes, beliefs and habits. Alternative behaviors must support new attitudes and habits. Therefore, your marketing efforts might rely upon some earlier survey/assessments related to health habits and program preferences.

BASIC STRATEGIES: THE FOUR P'S OF MARKETING

Developing a marketing/promotion plan is an integral part of the planning process. Four basic strategies, known in marketing as the "Four P's," should be considered in developing your promotional approach. These factors are Product, Placement, Promotion, and Pricing. The combination of these factors is also called the marketing mix.

P-1: PRODUCT

This strategy involves developing the right product for the targeted market. In health promotion, this means careful selection of programs based on an assessment of audience need, and, when marketing to organizations, what you can reasonably deliver. *Rapp and Collins (1987)* identified the five key product dimensions as: durability, complexity, visibility, risk and familiarity. By understanding these product dimensions and your target groups' characteristics, you can then construct the most effective HP services/products. Any product delivery should follow these general guidelines.

1. Make sure your product hits at least one large or two small, but fairly similar target audiences.

2. Keep the message about the features of your product up-beat and positive; do not use guilt, threats or intimidation to sell. Emphasize the benefits of smoking reduction, better nutrition or weight loss.

3. Try to give your product marketing a novel or humorous twist (Buns on the Run-- Safeway), but use ideas that are within the framework of the organization's culture.

4. Use a level of communication appropriate to the organization and your target audiences. Do not get too technical or complex unless the target groups' characteristics indicate that such an appeal is needed or will work effectively.

P-2: PLACEMENT

This strategy is concerned with getting the right product to the right marketplace. Where can the target audience most conveniently obtain the desired products or services (assessability/access). Placement requires us to also ask where the program should be located within the internal organization. How would it be perceived differently by employees as a function of benefits, personnel, employee relations, or health and safety, etc.? Or should it be delivered externally, utilizing the YMCA, local gym or health club, or via other community resources? How can it be linked to other places and services that will maximize exposure, acceptance, and accessibility to the target audience? For example, start a program on smoking that coincides with the Cancer Society's "Great American Smokeout," or link a nutrition program with a local health food company's nutrition display in the cafeteria. The following are Placement considerations:

1. **Location**--Access to the program can determine its success.

2. **Time**--The needs of the target audience will determine selection of the time of day, day of week, and time of year the program will be offered will be determined by needs of the target audience.

3. **Length**--Education and motivation components are usually lectures that last an hour or two. Intervention programs are usually multi-session activities.

4. **Exposure**--This applies to on-going programs, such as healthy cafeteria menus or a smoke-free environment that do not end, but must continually be promoted, monitored, accounted for, and evaluated.

5. **Integration**--This refers to the mix of programs that may be all going on at one time and the order in which they occur due to the nature of the content of each and inter-relationships.

P-3: PROMOTION

This strategy matches the target audience with the right product at the right place. This strategy most often comes to mind when one thinks of marketing. Promotion is exemplified by publicity, advertising, and sales techniques. In promoting a healthier lifestyle, we are trying to convince prospects that this program fills their existing needs, not trying to create one that does not exist. The questions and concerns of the following areas of promotion are also related to product development issues which must be answered: How are we going to position our product? How are we going to package, conceptualize, and communicate the strengths of our product? What niche in the market is it going to fill? Do we want to position it as "health at work" or as "personal wellness"? Do we want to position our program as a progressive thing that the company is doing for employees and is but a part of a total benefit package?

Advertising/Publicity/Media--Publicity can be structured in a variety of ways. We have already discussed some issues in previous sections of this chapter. The techniques for publicity and advertising are only limited by our own creative abilities. For example, we can publish messages in various company newsletters, making sure that the right message reaches the right target audience, or publish our own wellness newsletter. We might develop a literature display for the cafeteria, personnel area, or at entry to the health facilities. Finally, we want to be sure to take advantage of opportunities to speak at various scheduled meetings and assemblies to introduce a new HP program. Some additional ideas include the following:

1. Mail health or wellness information and publications (news-letter, magazine, poster, calender, HRA) to employees' homes to get the entire family involved.

2. Display motivational and general awareness type banners, posters and other messages in strategic places.

3. Put bullet-type, short health messages on cafeteria food, in payroll checks, on bumper stickers, calendars and catalogs.

4. Develop a colorful, distinctive HP logo and put it on everything associated with your activities, communications, and publicity.

Media activities are very important since they typically convey the message to more people at one time. Media ideas include the following:

1. Develop materials pertaining to upcoming media programs on TV or radio that relate to health topics and support the programs you are promoting.

2. Produce or purchase from outside vendors such media as films, videotapes, film-strips, audio tapes, and slide/tapes on health and wellness issues. Note that these are generally available for a 3-day preview at a low cost, and the preview price normally applies toward the rental or purchase price. Always preview media materials to make sure they are accurate, specific, non-threatening, motivating, and supportive of short-term learning goals and long-term HP system and program goals--as well as

being interesting, professionally presented, and appropriate to your audience. Then hold a preview session with your HP task force to be sure they agree with your impressions.

3. Create a press kit: A media information package that includes a program description, samples of announcements, open houses, current events, and articles from company publications or other local news media.

P-4: PRICING

This strategy focuses on determining the appropriatecost to promote and implement the program. It is often necessary in selecting health promotion programs to give thought to the organization's resources and the willingness of participants to pay for part or all of the program. To what extent to utilize consultants, outside medical services, or in-house personnel? There is always an exchange regarding some dimension of price, but it is not always money. Are you asking employees to spend time, or will work time be used for participation? What costs are you imposing on the employees? How can you make these exchanges satisfactory to your employees and to the organization (both parties)? Remember that time and freedom is a precious resource for many employees and companies, so programs must be promoted in a positive and soft manner, with participation optional and provide an explanation of their rationale and benefits. Also find out what the employees' expectations are regarding your HP program. What are they willing to invest in order to achieve the results.

TECHNIQUES FOR DETERMINING WHAT PEOPLE WANT

Informal communication--This is an outgrowth of the planning committee. When a health promotion committee member goes around to co-workers and asks them for feedback about a proposed program, this is an informal method of communication.

Paper and pencil and face-to-face interviews--This is a slightly more formal version of the one above. The planning committee member simply asks specific questions about and records coworkers' needs and interests. The results of these surveys are collated and analyzed

Participation rate--This technique calls for someone to monitor selective HP orientation events. Much is learned by what is said before, during, and after the event, as well as by how well the event is attended.

Focus groups--Approximately 10 to 12 people meet with a promotion/facilitator who will generate group interaction along certain dimensions. This strategy is often used in marketing. One example of this type of technique was used several years ago by the Department of Health and Human Services who brought owners of small business together and asked them: "What do small business want in the way of a health promotion program? This would be a valuable tool to get feedback from participants to get their suggestions for improving your product or service.

Task force--We discussed this type of session at great length in our chapter on planning. Please review that material if you need to do so and think of it from the marketing perspective.

SUMMARY
Professionals in the health promotion field have a great deal to learn from the marketing industry. Advertising that is directed at encouraging individuals to purchase products or engage in behaviors that are detrimental to their health is pervasive. Study the advertising methods of the tobacco, food, and alcohol industries and then adapt their methods to promote wellness through your HP program.

9

CONCLUSIONS AND HEALTH COST MANAGEMENT

INTRODUCTION

This chapter summarizes some final issues you will likely find relevant, whether operating as a health promotion consultant or working in some fashion with health promotion programs. We briefly address some of the more pertinent concepts and ideas pertaining to health care cost management. Many health promotion efforts have begun as a result of someone, usually at the top, becoming understandably concerned about the rapid rise in health care insurance premiums and other attendant costs. Many of these increases have been about 20% per year, or even greater. The more you can contribute to an educated discussion of cost containment (not that this should always be your primary goal) the more likely your services (and skills) will perceived as necessary to effective management of the organization.

HEALTH CARE COST MANAGEMENT ISSUES AND IMPLICATIONS FOR HEALTH PROMOTION PROGRAMS

The information that follows is designed will provide an introductory understanding of the issues pertaining to the topic of health care cost management and its relationship to building more effective, ongoing health promotion programs. As health costs have risen, management has become more attentive to the many ways to alleviate the impact of these costs.

THE HEALTH CARE DELIVERY SYSTEM

The health care delivery system refers to the loosely structured system of practitioners, facilities, institutions and programs that provide and finance health services. According to *Hall (et. al., 1984)* "the health care system has certain characteristics that are not often found, at least in combination, in most other economic systems." Hall cites the following to support this contention:

1. Health care is often thought of as a "right," irrespective of an individual's economic or social circumstance.

2. Providers and consumers tend to assume that more care is better care and that "doing" is better than "not doing." The practice of "defensive medicine," whereby physicians seek to reduce the risk of malpractice by increasing the number of tests and visits, accentuates this tendency.

3. Health services are offered by many providers serving local, not national markets. Innovations introduced in one area may not affect other areas.

4. There is limited coordination between providers, resulting in varying degrees of duplication of health care facilities, equipment, services and personnel.

5. Health services are both technology and labor-intensive, and are characterized by rapid technological advances, high labor costs and a high rate of equipment and facility obsolescence. One seldom finds an industry where advances in sophisticated technology is combined with increases in labor costs.

6. Health care providers compete vigorously to provide more status orientated, technologically sophisticated, diversified, and more profitable services.

7. Providers generally do not compete to furnish services at lower costs. Cost is usually not a major factor in determining what, how or where to buy, as long as the hospital or physician does not bear the expense.

8. Physicians make decisions that affect about 70% of all health expenditures. Patients have a relatively minor role in deciding what services to buy, in what quantity, and where to buy them.

9. Consumers are usually not in a position to make informed choices regarding the quantity and quality of services needed in the event of a sickness.

10. Parts of the health care delivery system are highly regulated. In some instances, it is difficult for new providers to enter the marketplace or experiment with different ways of delivering services.

11. Most payments for care are made by "third parties" (government, insurance, self-funded companies, etc.). Participants in health care transactions are thereby insulated from the direct, immediate economic consequences of their decisions.

THREE COST CONTAINMENT METHODS

Employers have pursued three distinctly different avenues in their attempts to moderate health cost escalation since it became a major concern in the early 1980s:

The first of these cost management measures is benefits redesign, which is one method that virtually all employers, large and small, have attempted. This has meant that employers have shifted some of the costs of health care to their employees through increased deductible amounts and co-payments. This has also meant a change in some of the ways that health care providers deliver their services.

The second cost containment method tried by many employers in pursuit of savings has been through selecting alternative delivery systems, particularly Health Maintenance Organizations (HMOs) and Preferred Provider Organizations (PPOs).However, early projections of huge cost savings for employers signing up for these plans have not materialized. Results of studies to determine their efficacy are mixed and somewhat controversial. *(See Herzlinger, Harvard Business Review, 1986)*

The third cost containment method is the one to which we have dedicated this book--health promotion. It is difficult to substantiate cost savings immediately and over the short-term,. so, it is important to create a more diversified rationale and couch some emerging positive evidence of cost savings with other substantial benefits.

HEALTH PROMOTION AS A COST-CONTAINMENT MEASURE

Many companies simply will not get involved in health promotion unless they can be reasonably sure that the overall effort will result in cost savings. It may be up to the HP consultant or professional's responsibility to set this issue in the proper perspective and time framework. First, the employer must realize that the workplace is an excellent environment for improving worker health. Research suggests some of the advantages of conducting health promotion at work include:

1. Convenience to the employees.
2. A higher rate of voluntary participation than in community programs.
3. A general feeling by employees that company-sponsored programs will be of high quality.
4. Peer group support for making difficult lifestyle changes.
5. The perception by employees of a valuable fringe benefit. *(Fielding, 1982)*

The potential bottom-line benefits for the company are a reduction in absenteeism, employee turnover, and health care costs, and an increase in productivity, employee fitness, and coping capability. Further, the company can demonstrate interest in their most valued resource--their employees. According to *Opatz (1985),* "health promotion activities, when combined with other health care cost containment measures, represent the best long-term answer for containing the rapid escalation of health care costs."

INDICATIONS FOR A HEALTH PROMOTION IMPERATIVE

Despite the strong trend toward wellness and personal accountability for health maintenance, the positive impact on the overall American workforce is slow in coming. Some of the statistics that have motivated companies of all sizes to develop an interest in promotion of health and cost containment are: Twenty-nine million work-days are lost annually due to hypertension, stroke, and coronary heart disease; thirty percent of the 100 million U.S. workers suffer from high blood pressure and are at risk for developing stroke, heart and kidney disease; about 26% of the U.S. population still smokes, and smokers have a much higher risk for many diseases. About 10 million employees (10%) suffer from alcoholism.

Some of the dollar amounts are equally astounding. At the current rate of increase, health care costs in the U.S. will amount to 20% of the gross national product (GNP) by 1993, or one trillion dollars! Health care now consumes over one out of every nine dollars the average worker earns, and employees work over one month each year to pay these costs. In 1983, medical expenditures averaged $1,459 per person, a record high. Employers now pay half of the nation's health bill, which accounts for 10% of the total compensation to employees. Companies are now spending over $700 million annually to replace more than 200,000 men between the ages of 45 and 65 who are killed or disabled by coronary heart disease. And finally, medical experts estimate that 70% of illness is preventable. *(Gutknecht, 1988)*

The following sections will briefly highlight some the issues important in benefits redesign. and present additional data to demonstrate the extent that health care costs have negatively impacted employers. These are important considerations since most comprehensive health promotion efforts conducted by companies will include a close look at the health care benefits package. The health promotion coordinator/consultant should have a basic understanding of the issues in this area.

THE HIGH COST OF EMPLOYEE ILLNESS AND INJURY
Several decades ago the cost of health care was taken for granted, and there was no need to be concerned with cost management. The economic realities of the 1970s and the 1980s however, have demanded that systematic approaches to containing health care costs be designed and implemented. Since employer-sponsored benefit plans represent more than 80% of the medical coverage in the United States, employers' ability to demand realistic and meaningful changes in the way health care is financed is substantial. Ultimately, it is the employers who pay the insurance companies and third parties.

The issue of spiraling health care costs and how to bring them down has been addressed in recent years by every sector of the economy. In 1983 the federal government introduced the concept of prospectively paid diagnostic-related groups (DRGs) to the Medicare and Medicaid systems. The DRG concept lengthened the period of time during which older employees and their spouses must be covered under employer-provided health insurance programs rather than Medicare. Unfortunately, in indirect ways, DRGs have shifted a larger portion of the health care burden to business and industry.

Employee Benefits Continue to Grow--In the private sector, it is rare to find an employer who has not expressed some interest in reducing health care costs in some manner. Employee benefits, fueled by rising health care costs, are continuing to comprise a larger and larger portion of employees' total compensation. According to the *U.S. Chamber of Commerce*, employers are spending more than $7,500 a year per employee for benefits. The sharp rise in health care costs in 1984 caused premiums to rise in over 90% of all U.S. industrial companies. According to a *Hay/Huggins Benefit Comparison Survey (1985)*, the average increase in employee premium from 1983 to 1984 was 18%, with almost two-thirds of the companies surveyed having premium increases of 15% or more. This 18% increase is much lower than the average rate of 26% reported between 1982 and 1983, and the 31% reported between 1981 and 1982.

CURRENT TRENDS IN COST CONTAINMENT

Several surveys conducted by benefits consulting firms such as *William M. Mercer*, show that many American companies have utilized some cost containment strategies in the past few years, although large companies are doing this more often than in the smaller businesses. It is encouraging to note that employers are taking the cost problem seriously, but most understand that there is no quick fix for the problems at hand. In fact, some cost control programs were found to be not very effective in the short term.

COST CONTAINMENT SURVEYS

A survey by *Towers, Perrins, Forster, and Crosby (1982)* found that among those companies included in their survey, cost containment efforts such as claims audits, voluntary second opinion programs, and pre-admission testing appeared to cost as much as they saved. Conversely, hospice care benefits, coinsurance, deductibles, and coordination of benefits (COB) generated significant savings. In their efforts to contain costs, employers are trying to involve their employees in cost containment efforts. One method is cost shifting, which shifts more of the cost to employees. The rationale is that as employees become more aware of the costs associated with medical care, they will become more cost conscious regarding such care.

Health Research Institute Survey

The *Health Research Institute* (HRI) has conducted biennial surveys of health care cost containment efforts by 1,500 companies since 1979. The 1983 results are based on 602 respondents (40.1%). HRI's report contains aggregate results and in some cases details on actual company practices. Some of the conclusions are presented below.

Increased Deductibles--Over one-third of the responding employers have increased deductible, and nearly 20% have increased coinsurance, stop-loss limits, and employee/dependent payroll contributions.

Alternative Delivery Systems--Over two-thirds of the companies polled offer an alternative delivery system (HMO or PPO) to their employees.

Second Opinions--Almost three-fourths of the companies use second opinions for surgery.

Outpatient Incentives--Employee incentives increase the usie of outpatient facilities. These incentives include waiving the deductibles and coinsurance, providingoutpatient bonuses and medical expense accounts.

Review of Charges--Over half of the employers encourage employees to review hospital bills to be sure they are not being charged for services or items they did not receive.

Kentucky Employers Handbook on Health Insurance Management Strategies
One of the most comprehensive reviews of the effectiveness of various cost containment measures is presented in the *Kentucky Employers Handbook on Health Insurance Management Strategies.* It suggests the cost savings potential of diverse strategies based on various studies and employee reports.

Massachusetts Business Roundtable Survey
This survey of five major health care insurers by the Massachusetts Business Roundtable Health Care Task Force illustrates the possible savings to employers who implement one or more of the design changes suggested on the following pages. Not many years ago, only a few of the options presented in these surveys were even available to employers. Now, it is rare when a company does not feature most of these in their benefits package.

RANGE OF POSSIBLE SAVINGS FROM
VARIOUS COST CONTAINMENT MEASURES

COST CONTAINMENT OPTION	Gross Reduction in Total Health Benefits Costs
Hospital utilization controls	
1. Second opinion surgery	1.0 to 4.0%
2. Ambulatory surgery	0.5 to 2.0%
3. Utilization review	4.0 to 4.1%
4. Pre-admission testing	1.0 to 2.0%
5. Pre-admission review	1.0 to 2.0%
Cost-sharing and cost shifting	
1. Deductibles	5.8% and up
2. Co-payments	13.0% and up
3. 24 hour maternity	$260 to 248 net savings per patient
Cost-effective health insurance benefits	
1. Home health care	0 to 1.0%
2. Hospice	1.1%
3. Birthing centers	0.2%
Expanding employee choice	
1. Health Maintenance Organization (HMO)	8.5 to 20% *
2. Preferred Provider Organization (PPO)	5.0 to 30%

(Adapted from Kentucky Employers Handbook on Health Insurance Management Strategies, March 1984).

MASSACHUSETTS BUSINESS ROUNDTABLE SURVEY

AMOUNT OF DEDUCTIBLE	PROJECTED SAVINGS
Front-end deductible for each insured plan member:	
$ 100	7.2%
300	4.7%
500	20.8%
Front end co-insurance provisions for each plan member:	
10%	8.5%
20%	17.0%
30%	27.5%

Co-insurance provisions with no major medical out-of-pocket maximum:

90%	3.6%
10%	12.0%
70%	17.9%

Front end deductible for room and board only:

$ 300	5.2%

Co-insurance provisions for surgery, percentage of reasonable and customary charges:

90%	1.2%
80%	2.8%
70%	4.3%

Individual or family major medical deductible requirements:

$ 100 indiv. or 300 family	2.7%
250 indiv. or 750 family	5.4%
500 indiv. or 1000 family	8.1%

AMOUNT OF DEDUCTIBLE	PROJECTED SAVINGS

Coverage for mental health or nervous disorders, percentage of payment with $500 maximum benefit:

100%	1.8%
80%	2.2%
50%	2.5%

Co-insurance provisions for lab or X-ray, percentage of reasonable and customary charges:

90%	0.4%
80%	0.8%
70%	1.3%

Limit per day on room and board:

$ 200	.0%

Out-of pocket maximums for each calendar year:

$1,000	0.5%
2,500	0.6%
5,000	0.7%

Lifetime maximum benefit limit:

$500,000	.05%
250,000	.07%

(Adapted from the Massachusetts Business Roundhouse Report, May, 1983.)

EMPLOYERS MUST CHANGE THEIR BENEFITS PACKAGES

Careful planning and considerations of all available and feasible options should do much to mitigate or eliminate costly miscalculations. The road to cost containment is long and hard, but so is the alternative--not confronting the issue. It is important to separate the forest from the trees, i.e., to get your goals and priorities straight and aligned with the organization's vision and mission problem areas are addressed, time and resources are not wasted on low-cost cosmetic items. When designing cost containment strategies, employers should first consider those cost initiatives that influence the greatest amount of expenditures *(Finkel, 1985)*. The table below illustrates the distribution of claims by claims level.

DISTRIBUTION OF CLAIMS AND INSURED EXPENDITURES, BY CLAIMS LEVEL

Expenditures	% of Total Claims Level	%of Total Number of Claims
$ 0 to 499	78%	14%
500 to 999	9%	8%
1000 to 4999	9%	33%
5000 to 9999	3%	24%
10,000 and over	1%	21%

(Adapted from the Massachusetts Business Roundhouse Report, May, 1983.)

This table indicates that 80% of dollars spent on health care are for treatments in excess of $1,000, and almost one-half of all expenditures are for treatments in excess of $5,000. To state the problem another way, treatments costing over $1,000 comprise 13% of the total claims but represent 78% of the total expenditures. Treatments costing less than $1,000 comprise 87% of claims and constitute about 22% of expenditures.

PLANNING THE BENEFITS REDESIGN EFFORT

According to *Walter McClure (1983)*, president of the Center for Policy Studies, employers usually focus first on better benefit and financial administration through improved claims review, coordination of benefits, and self-funding. These actions, although important, mainly affect administrative costs, which only represent 5 to 10% of the benefit program expenses. The remaining 90 to 95% of costs are untouched. Wellness programs, pre-admission testing, deductible and co-insurance increases, mandatory second opinion programs, and utilization review are some important next steps that should be considered. *McClure* mentions using consumer incentives to reduce costs, such as bonuses for healthy lifestyles, deductibles for service usage, and selection of a PPO or an HMO. He points out however, that these employee incentives that are intended to reduce employee usage of services have limited cost savings because they frequently are services which cost less than $1,000. Expensive procedures costing more than $1,000 comprise about 78% of medical claims. Thus much of the cost containment effort, he feels, should focus on provider incentives, which will effect the greatest cost savings in the immediate future.

To address the long-term real cost problem,, employers must address the behavior pattern of their employees and, to a larger extent, influence provider behavior. Incentive reimbursements to employees and providers should be offered in an effort to hold down prices and costs and to curb excessive use of services. More efficient and responsible, peer-reviewed medical practice styles should be initiated and promoted. The basic objectives of plan redesign are to encourage economical and effective use of health care by employees and to restrict the use of those benefits of which the appropriateness or necessity is questionable. Flexibility is an important ingredient in stabilizing employer costs. A well-thought out plan can significantly influence utilization patterns and costs. An important consideration in plan design is how much to ask the employee to involve themselves and to contribute. How can we foster system-wide involvement, ownership and participation? What are acceptable deductible and co-insurance rates? What effect does cost sharing have upon spending?

Finkel (1985) outlines some of the key steps to aid in the redesign process:

1. Identify employer philosophy regarding employee benefits.
2. Develop guidelines and policies; set levels of benefits.
3. Elicit employees' thoughts and attitudes regarding benefits coverage.
4. Implement the new plan with a clear communication strategy.
5. Publicize the benefits package periodically; educate employees about cost conscious behavior.
6. Evaluate the plan to assess how well it is meeting intended objectives. Monitor utilization of the most costly components.

CONTAIN COSTS WITH DEDUCTIBLES AND CO-INSURANCE

A deductible is a stipulated sum that the covered individual must pay toward the cost of health treatment before the benefits of the program go into effect. Co-insurance, or co-payment is the provision of a program in which the insured shares in the cost of covered services on a percentage basis. A typical co-insurance arrangement is 80/20, i.e., the carrier pays 80% of the benefit and the employee pays the difference. These percentages vary from plan to plan. In the good old days, most plans had a $50 to $100 deductible and paid 100% of the co-insurance. Those plans provided incentives for misuse, and individuals were not encouraged or motivated to use the least cost effective or even most preventive health care alternatives. Most new plans have increased the deductible and more companies have lowered the co-insurance rate. Deductibles that encourage the use of more costly care should be eliminated. Most plans also have a maximum out-of-pocket ceiling.

COST BENEFITS OF SHARING COSTS WITH EMPLOYEES

The Rand corporation prepared one of the largest, most comprehensive studies conducted on the effects of cost sharing and spending for medical care. Almost 8,000 individuals in six states were studied up to five years. The purpose was to find out the effects of insurance for factors that might or might not be covered in possible national health insurance plans. The Rand research studied the effects of adopting different co-insurance schedules: 95% co-insurance, family deductible; 95% co-insurance, individual deductible; 50% co-insurance; 25% co-insurance, group health, experimental group; and group health controls. The maximum dollar expenditure out of pocket was $1,000 or some percent of family income. The initial analysis showed that cost sharing clearly lowered total spending, that is patients sought care for fewer illnesses. Although the economic results of the Rand study are favorable, judgments about cost containment must be held in abeyance until more research is completed. Do patients who use fewer health services because they have large co-payments also have poorer health? There is some concern about this issue among those who study HMOs. Also, simply raising the co-payments and deductibles in benefit plans will not necessarily solve the problems. The medical system reacts by raising its rates and, in many cases, forgives the patient for the additional deductible and co-insurance rates.

Unfortunately there is no unanimity of opinion as to what constitutes a cost effective package. What may work for one organization may not necessarily work for another. Ideally, cost containment should be encouraged while adequate coverage is provided; any reduction in coverage in one area should be balanced by improvements in another. The overriding objectives should be to provide a more rational set of benefits for a similar amount of money and to make these benefits more resistant to inflation. Simplicity is a key ingredient. Benefits redesign is a complex process requiring the consumer and the provider cooperate and work together. Like so many areas of modern organizational life, we must build good communication linkages and skills, and the more effective linkage of vision, mission and goals if we are to solve these problems.

NEW ISSUES FOR EMPLOYERS

It appears that while individual employers are reporting savings as a result of their health care cost containment programs, the general picture is that cost containment efforts have only been successful in slowing the rate of cost increase, but not in lowering health costs, or even keeping them even. As the efforts toward cost containment continue, it is appropriate to note one important additional factor--the steps that are being taken to solve the cost increase problem are giving rise to new issues. The consequences of any solution may create additional consequences which also must be carefully monitored.

NEWSLETTERS

Employee Health and Fitness--This is a monthly, 12-page newsletter that emphasizes current developments in the field of employee health promotion. Descriptions of company programs, a regular resource column, and discussion of program areas are included. Specific advise on design and development of company programs is a regular feature. (Employee Health and Fitness, 67 Peachtree Park Drive, Atlanta, GA 30309).

Worksite Wellness Works--Published by the Wellness Council of America, it focuses on organizing wellness programs in the workplace. Published in Omaha, Nebraska, it is backed by the Insurance Corporation of America.

University of California, Berkeley Wellness Letter--Published by the Public Health Department at the University of California--Berkeley, P.O. Box 359148, Palm Coast, Florida 32035. It is a monthly, consumer newsletter focusing on nutrition, fitness, and stress management.

Nutrition Action Newsletter--Published by CSPI, 1501 16 th St. N. W., Washington, D.C. 20036-1499, a nonprofit public interest organization that advocates improved health and environmental policies.

Hospital and Employee Health is published monthly by American Health Consultants, 67 Peachtree Park Drive, NE, Atlanta GA 30309.

JOURNALS

Physician and Sports Medicine--This is a monthly journal that often includes articles of specific interest to worksite fitness program coordinators. (Physician and Sports Medicine, McGraw-Hill Publishing Co., 1221 Avenue of the Americas, New York, New York, 10020.)

American Journal of Health Promotion--A new publication devoted totally to the field of health promotion. The address is 746 Purdy Street, Birmingham, Michigan 48009.

Journal of Occupational Health--Journal emphasizes workplace safety and health issues and is written for the practicing workplace health professionals.

American Journal of Public Health--A technical journal for public health professionals. Many articles deal with health promoting subjects.

American Journal of Preventive Medicine--A professional medical journal dealing with all aspects of prevention.

Journal of Clinical and Consulting Psychology

New England Journal of Medicine

Social Science and Medicine

Annals of Behavioral Medicine

Journal of Primary Prevention

Advances in Environmental Psychology

Public Health Reviews

Journal of Health and Social Behavior

Journal of Compliance in Health Care

RESOURCE ORGANIZATIONS

The Wellness Councils of America (WELCOA)--Dedicated to providing information, direction and support services to community-based Wellness Councils. Its mission is to share resources and information that allow organizations to promote healthier lifestyles for their workers. The insurance industry has been an active participant and supporter of this movement (Historic Library Plaza,1823 Harney Street., Suite 201, Omaha, Nebraska 68102).

The American Society for Healthcare Education and training--This organization is part of the American Hospital Association's effort to encourage health promotion activities among hospitals. The center provides a regular newsletter, "Promotion Health" and can handle inquiries about local hospital and community programs. (Center for Health Promotion, American Hospital Association, 840 North Lake Shore Drive, Chicago, Ill 60611).

American College of Preventive Medicine--A clearinghouse for information on health promotion programs. Information is available concerning model programs in the workplace. (1015 15th Street, N.W., Suite 403, Wash. D.C., 20005).

National Health Information Clearinghouse--This agency answers inquiries by telephone or mail about most health-related questions and refers individuals making inquiries to the appropriate references or organizations. The clearinghouse also publishes a directory to health information resources in the U.S. Department of Health and Human Services, an inventory of risk hazard appraisals, a guide to fitness organizations, and other materials. (National Health Information Clearinghouse, 1555 Wilson Boulevard, Rosslyn, Virginia, 22209).

Office of Health Information, Health Promotion and Physical Fitness, and Sports Medicine--This is the focal in the U.S. Department of Health and Human Services for health promotion activities. Although the office is concerned with a variety of settings, the workplace is a key interest. The office has sponsored a national conference on health promotion at the workplace is a key interest. (Office of the Assistant Secretary for Health, U.S. Department of Health and Human Services, Washington, D.C., 20201).

The American College of Sports Medicine--Information on endurance testing and certification of exercise leaders. (1440 Monroe Street, Madison, Wisconsin 53706).

American Occupational Medical Association--Conducts educational conferences in occupational medicine and is the largest society of physicians in industry, government, and academia who promote the health of workers in industry. Services include surveillance of harmful substances, alcoholic rehabilitation, and employment referral for physicians interested in occupational medicine (150 North Wacker Drive, Chicago, Ill., 60606).

American Public Health Association--Devoted to the promotion of public health for its members (50,000 plus) and the concerned public. Sets standards for solving health problems, sponsors large public awareness campaigns about specific health dangers(1015 18th Street, N.W., Washington D.C., 20036).

Washington Business Group on Health--Provides publications, research reports, legislation trends, and consultations to individuals and organizations in the area of health promotion programs in occupational settings. (922 Pennsylvania Ave. S.E., Washington D.C., 20003).

American Association of Occupational Health Nurses--Dedicated to the promotion of occupational health nursing , and health promotion, wellness, right-to-know for patients, confidentiality of employee health records, and health cost management (3500 Piedmont Rd., Suite 400, Atlanta, Georgia 30305).

National Wellness Association--This nonprofit organization is dedicated to meet the growing needs of wellness professionals for information, services, and networking opportunities (University of Wisconsin-Stevens Point, Stevens Point, Wisconsin 54481).

Association for the Advancement of Health Education-- Provides professional services and information regarding health promotion and general health topics to members in such fields as clinical, community health, and school settings (1900 association Drive, Reston, Virginia 22091)

The Society for Prospective Medicine--Devoted innovative and progressive means of studying, implementing, and intervening in the natural history of disease to improve the useful life expectancy of the public (P.O. Box 20548, Indianapolis, Indiana 46220-0548).

Society for Public Health Education--It is dedicated to the field of heath education through the setting of ethical standards of practice, and providing a wider access for good health education research (2001 Addison Street, Suite 220, Berkeley, Ca. 94704).

American Association of Fitness Directors in Business and Industry--This is a membership organization of more than 1500 people involved in some phase of workplace health. The association, founded in 1974, is affiliated with the President's Council on Physical Fitness and Sports. A quarterly newsletter, annual conference, and a job clearinghouse are among its activities.

SPECIAL TOPICS AND TRENDS
Facilitating AIDS Education in the Workplace. According to C. Everett Koop, Surgeon General, "This manual is comprehensive and well designed and will facilitate industry efforts to contain the spread of HIV infection. Underwritten by The Pacific Mutual Life Insurance Company, this booklet can be obtained at no cost by simply calling this Newport Beach Company at (800) 544-3600.

Stress Management:
American Institute of Stress--This institute is devoted to the multi-disciplinary study of the relationship between stress and illness. It acts as a clearinghouse of information and programs in the areas of stress and wellness (124 Park Avenue, Yonkers, N.Y.,10703).

Physical Fitness:
Participation--An exceptional organization which provides a packet of materials entitled, "Fitness: The Facts. This is a six-part series of colorful and accurate brochures on physical fitness. (Director of Marketing, 80 Richmond Street West, Suite 805, Toronto, Ontario, M4H 2A4, Canada).

Toxic Substance Control and Environmental Protection:
Chicago Area Committee on Occupational Safety and Health (CACOSH)--The first and one of the most successful of the COSH groups. A coalition of

trade unions and health and legal workers, it provides a variety of organizing functions for trade unionists and unorganized workers. (542 South Dearborn Street, Chicago, Ill. 60605.)

Alcohol and Chemical Abuse:

National Institute on Alcohol Abuse and Alcoholism and National Institute on Drug Abuse--This agency was established by the federal government to initiate research and prevention programs concerning alcoholism and drug abuse. (Public Health Service, 5600 Fisher Lane, Rockville, Maryland, 20857) *Alcoholics Anonymous, Al-Anon Family Groups, Adult Children of Alcoholics, and Narcotics Anonymous*--(National, Non-profit, self-help groups are listed in local yellow pages).

High Blood Pressure Control:

National High Blood Pressure Education Program--Offers a work-setting kit especially for industry which includes instructional materials and information for distribution; also has consultants and other resources. (120/80 National Institute of Health, Bethesda, MD, 20014).

Weight Control:

(National For-Profit and non-profit programs include): Overeaters Anonymous, Weight Watchers, The Diet Center.

Smoking Cessation:

American Lung Association--The goal of the association is the prevention and control of lung diseases. They offer patient services, school programs, educational materials and teacher-training workshops. Offered free to the public are a vast array of quit-smoking kits, pamphlets, buttons, and brochures. (Local chapters in most large metropolitan areas).

National Cancer Institute--Established in 1937 as part of the Public Health Service, this is the federal government's principal agency for cancer research and prevention programs. The goal of the institute is the reduction and eventual elimination of cancer as a major health problem.

APPENDIX 2 :CASE STUDY

INTRODUCTION:

The following case study is actually a composite of a number of companies with whom the authors have consulted in the last five years. While the company is fictitious, the information we have provided is designed to elicit a number of important issues that are pertinent and sometimes controversial. We hope that this material will provide an opportunity for practical application of the principles we discuss from week-to-week. You will use this information about this company to form opinions about how this organization should tackle the development, design and implementation of a health promotion program.

We recommend that you divide into small groups for discussion of this case study. Following this discussion period each group will be asked to address one or more specific issues and give a small report to the class as a whole.

Company Name: Acme Chemical Co.

Company Industry: Chemical Industry

Major products sold or service provided: Pesticides and fertilizers

Company size (annual sales, number of employees): Annual sales are currently $25 million. The company has 500 employees. They have a small production line and a large warehouse where chemicals are stored before shipment. About 40% of the workforce is blue collar and 35% is female.

Company location: Anywhere U.S.A.

Financial trends: Slow, steady growth despite being in an industry under siege. They are becoming more and more regulated, with liability and insurance costs skyrocketing. Some hope for an increase in international sales due to sinking dollar.

Company policy toward the management of human resources: Upper management has emphasized training and development of the management staff for several years and has provided means for making that possible. They have not actively promoted health in the workplace as yet.

Management philosophy and corporate style. This has been a family owned and dominated business during its 20 years of existence. Recently, the founder has retired leaving his son as the new CEO. Most employee, see this as a positive change. The new CEO is said to be much more in tune with the way companies should be run today. He delegates responsibility better and is much more responsive to change than the previous CEO. Some believe that the company should recruit additional professional management and use more outside consultants.

The corporate culture (core values, beliefs, etc.--see chapter 2) is good, despite some vestiges of negative attitudes left over from the previous leadership. Good communication from upper management regarding the company's mission and goals has become apparent since the change in CEO. Employees seem to feel he is someone who cares about them as well as the bottom line. They are just beginning to understand the importance of health promotion and its relationship to better utilization of health care resources. Yet, the company seems to lacks a basic knowledge about health promotion and how it is effectively implemented. Management feels they are too regulated.

Salient facts about company history: This company sells manufactured products to the end user. As a chemical company they feel embattled and somewhat vulnerable to the increasing environmental issues that will not go away. Errors and the poor reputation of others in their industry have also effected them. As a result, a variety of expenses have skyrocked. They find it hard to get insurance of any kind, but particularly health and liability. They are concerned about their future.

Events that triggered interest in health promotion program: Due to recent problems in the industry (one was a fire at a chemical manufacturing plant that released a vapor cloud into a residential community), they are considered a high risk. They could find only one company interested in underwriting their insurance, and this company will only consider them if they buy all their insurance through them (this includes medical).

This insurance company has inquired about the state of health of the workforce generally and is considering this in its final decision. Their decision is about seven weeks away. The CEO has no health or other vital organizational information at his fingertips, other than the increased annual premiums and rates for various insurance policies Health insurance premiums have increased an average of 20% per year over the last four years.

Also, a key employee died recently of a heart attack at the age of 46 and several warehouse workers have seriously injured their backs and have been on worker's compensation for three months to one year. The union is also threatening to strike if a HMO is offered as the sole alternative.

Persons responsible for initiating interest in health promotion: CEO acting on the suggestion of the HR manager.

Their stated reasons for this exploration: Cost containment. They are unsure of but interested in other reasons why health promotion is important. Basically they lack information.

CASE STUDY QUESTIONS FOR SMALL GROUP DISCUSSION
Before the CEO authorizes a health promotion program, he wants to understand more about this field as it relates to his company. He asks your department (or your consulting firm) to prepare a brief report addressing:

1) What the terms "wellness" and "health promotion" actually mean for hi business; also, what is the rationale for various types of health promotion programs and which ones might be created to help his company immediately?

2) Why the company could benefit from a health promotion program even though we already has a medical/insurance plan?

3) Why are employees more likely to be successful in making positive lifestyle changes through the participation in a greater number of company-sponsored programs than through various ones located in the community or traditional medicine?

Briefly detail below the issues you would present in this report. Also discuss what information you do not possess at this time but would like to know more about.

1. Based on the preliminary information presented, what factors do you think may work for and against the successful development of a health promotion program in this company?

2. Do you feel the reason suggested by the CEO for exploring the possibility of a health promotion program is valid? Why?

CONTINUING CASE STUDY

We have determined that if the right conditions are present, upper management will actively support a health promotion program. However, in this situation, the CEO of Acme Chemical Co. is new and does not want to make a wrong (or hasty) decision that might cost the company money, time, and other important resources .Accordingly, the CEO has asked your department (or your consulting team) to conduct a feasibility study.

Important Facts About a Health Promotion Feasibility Study

The goal of a feasibility study is to determine the appropriateness of developing a health promotion program by examining the variables that are critical to its successful operation. A feasibility study is useful for the following reasons: 1) It can be performed quickly and inexpensively; 2) It can prevent investment of funds in a project that the study predicts would not be successful; 3) It provides much of the basic research information that is required for the design of a health promotion program; and 4) It permits early contact with many other departments and individuals that will be important to a successfully designed and effectively run program.

The three phases of a feasibility study are:

1. **Research**--Interviews with key managers and employees, examination of relevant organizational statistics, examination of current facilities, and survey of accessible community resources.

2. **Analysis**--Integration and analysis of all information collected.

3. **Report**--Written discussion of all the issues considered, oral presentations of major points, and question and answer session.

Additional Facts About Acme Chemical Co.:

In surveying managers for the feasibility study, the following findings emerge:
1. The managers feel that absenteeism is too high, and the continuity of management and resulting production is adversely affected by it. Although sickness is the most commonly cited reason given by employees who are absent from work, some managers notice that other type problems are also responsible.

2. Employees have expressed some concern about the toxicity of the chemicals that they are sometimes exposed to. They feel the company may not be telling them the whole story. General safety appears to be lax.

3. Turnover is relatively high among blue collar workers.

4. Some managers are wary of the potential distractions posed by creating a major health promotion system due to previous short-lived development programs. Managers of blue collar workers want to know if workers will be pulled off line to participate.

5. Upper management has agreed (CEO and CFO) that if the arguments are persuasive, particularly related to the financial benefits of a health promotion

system, they will provide the funding necessary to get it going. Is this enough commitment?

6. Besides the skyrocketing health premiums, the company has recently had a worker's compensation claim filed based upon the assertion of job-related stress. This person joins two other employees who have recently filed because of lower-back problems.

CASE STUDY ISSUES FOR SMALL GROUP DISCUSSION
For each of the issues listed below that are usually addressed by a feasibility study, answer the following questions. (If you feel you do not have sufficient information about Acme Chemical Co., make up something that will show your understanding of the issue involved.):

Organizational Goals and Motives
A. Why is the organization considering developing health promotion system?

B. What does your organization hope to gain from the development of such a program?

Cost Versus Benefit Aspects
A. Is development of a health promotion system a cost-effective method for supporting the stated goals of the organization?

B. What are the general categories of expenses for developing and operating the HP system and individual programs?

C. What are the current employee categories that may be positively affected by a health promotion program?

D. What are the probable benefits that the organization can hope to achieve through a health promotion system?

E. How do costs and benefits compare? Does a health promotion program appear to be a good use of the organization's resources?

Organizational and Community Capabilities

A. Is the organization capable of developing a health promotion system, assuming that there has been a positive costs versus benefit analysis?

B. What is the level of support for a H P system or specific programs among key management personnel and other employees?

C. What is the availability of resources in the organization and the community that are necessary for the development and operation of a health promotion system, including knowledge of the concept, facilities, staff, and financing?

Program Development Aspects

A. If creating a health promotion system seems a good investment of the organization's resources and the organization can obtain all the necessary resources either internally or from the community, how should the organization proceed in developing specific programs?

B. What will be the major obstacles in developing these programs?

C. What departments and individuals should be involved in developing these programs?

D. What are the various combinations of community and organizational resources that can be used to develop programs?

E. What kinds of programs seem most appropriate for achieving the stated goals of the H P system?

CONTINUING CASE STUDY

Additional Facts About Acme Chemical Co.: The health promotion planning committee has begun their health promotion program with a health risk appraisal. The HRA data can be used to assess personal and company health status at this time, and it will provide important data for evaluating program effectiveness at some future date.

The data from the HRA, a wellness inventory, and an employee needs and interest survey revealed the following:

Employee Health Profile:
1. A high percentage of smokers (35%).
2. 25% of workforce with borderline or high blood pressure.
3. A low percentage of the female workers conduct a breast self-exam.
4. 5% admit to drinking heavily (more than 14 per week)
5. 30% of workforce use seat belts less than 75% of the time.
6. 5% of workforce believe they should be better coping with stress.
7. 15% of the workforce are more than 20% overweight.
8. 35% of the workforce have a risk (appraised) age that is higher than their actual age.

What the employees say they want in the way of health promotion activities [ranked in order of their preference:

1. Weight loss program
2. Exercise programs (aerobics, fitness equipment)
3. Stress Management
4. Time Management
5. Nutrition

Little or no interest was expressed in the following activities:

1. Back injury prevention
2. Smoking cessation
3. Hypertension program
4. Driving safety
5. Alcohol education

In matching the goals expressed by the company with specific health promotion activities desired by the employees it becomes apparent that some major marketing efforts will be needed. The planning committee with some additional input from various levels of management has decided upon the following programs listed the following:

1. Stop smoking policy coupled with an on-site cessation program.
2. Hypertension management program
3. Back injury prevention
4. Nutrition education and management

5. Policy for safe driving when using company autos.
6. Incentives to help employees quit smoking
7. Incentives (or rewards) to help employees feel they have some ownership of the program.
8. Friendly competition between departments.

With these facts in mind, answer the following questions:

1. How would you implement any of these programs? (Briefly describe the materials needed, the staffing, the timetable for the various components included in this event, and any other relevant logistics.)

2. Since an obvious difference exists between what the employees want and what the company needs, how would you help reconcile the two health promotion constituents?

3. Design a simple flowchart to show how you would implement a health promotion program in this company. Include specific events that fall under the following categories: assessment/ testing, education/motivation, workshops, and adaptation (company policies).

4. Describe some workplace incentive programs that might be effective for: 1) increasing participation in health promotion activities, and 2) increasing success rate in behavior change programs.

CONTINUING CASE STUDY
ADDITIONAL FACTS ABOUT ACME CHEMICAL CO. A small committee was formed to oversee the evaluation effort. You are a committee member and your report to the larger task force committee. must address the following issues:

One of the committee's first jobs was to to decide what type of smoking cessation program was needed. They have narrowed the selection down to two programs. The committee was then asked to determine which one would be more cost effective in the long term and which one they recommended.

The first program (Program X) is a non-profit, agency-based program costing fifty five dollars per employee. The program has a published one year success-rate of 32%.

The second program (Program Y) isoften by a for-profit health promotion company. Their program costs $200 per employee, but has a one year success-rate of 52%.

The employee will pay for whichever program is chosen. If Program Y is chosen, the company has agreed to allow a payroll deduction for those not able to pay the $200 up front. The entire fee for the chosen program will be reimbursed to all employees who successfully quit for six months.

The evaluation committee, after surveying the literature, has determined that $1500 is the average extra cost to employ a smoker versus a nonsmoker at Acme Chemical Co. They consider this a middle-ground estimate, since some authoritative studies have calculated figures as high as $4600 per smoker, per year.

1. Which of the two programs do you feel would be most cost effective for Acme Chemical to implement (If all costs except the one stated above are equal)?

2. What considerations do you feel should go into the decision-making process for Acme's smoking cessation program?

Measurements taken during the Health Risk Appraisal indicated that 25% of those participating in this health event had borderline high blood pressure to high blood pressure (hypertension). The evaluation committee speculates that the incidence of hypertension is at least as great in the remaining portion of the workforce.

While the health professionals were able to recommend that many of these employees see their physicians, the committee concluded that a workplace hypertension program will be the best way to approach the problem. The comprehensive program recommended would have the following components: 1) prevention (open to all employees and is primarily focused on stress management); 2) motivation and goal-setting; 3) education; 4) workshops (to include skill-building, behavior change, medical compliance, stress management, and follow-up aspects); and 5) cultural and policy support.

The company has made a one year commitment to this program.
Studies indicate that health insurance claims, and health care costs, increase in the first 12 months for those employees seeking treatment through a workplace hypertension program.

With these facts in mind, please answer the following questions:

1. What do you feel would be some realistic goals for this program component?

2. What summative evaluation measures might you implement for this program component?

3. What formative evaluation measures might you employ for this program component?

CONTINUING CASE STUDY
Acme Chemical Co. is now faced with a number of problems that require marketing solutions. Please address the following:

Discussion point #1
A survey of reasons why the smoking employees of Acme Chemical Co. wanted to quit smoking listed the following reasons in order of frequency:

1. It's a dirty habit.
2. I don't want to smell like cigarettes any more.
3. I want to look and feel younger.
4. I know it's bad for me.
5. I want to live longer.

A large number of smokers indicated they wanted to quit and would consider a program offered at the workplace, since a smoke-free workplace policy is about to be enacted:1. Is there any reason to think that a smoking cessation program may not be successful?

2. How would you consider promoting (publicize and advertise) a kickoff event?

Discussion Point #2
A needs and interest survey indicates that the employees do not know what the risk factors are for continuing smoking. It seems that such a lack of information and awareness could results in low participation rates in any smoking program adopted.

1) How might you bridge this information gap, and 2) how would you conduct the program differently if a large contingent of lifetime smokers were indicated in your assessments?

Discussion Point #3
While a weight reduction program is not a high management priority, an employee survey indicates it is strongly desired. Further data indicates that the employees have a strong preference for any program designed to help them lose weight quickly. Research indicates that weight that is lost quickly is almost impossible to keep off.

As the key program planner or consultant, what would you do?

Discussion Point #4
You have just sold your employer on the benefits of a wellness program by appealing to his "hot button," i.e., that health promotion can increase his productivity and contain health care costs. This will save him money. Your first assignment is a feasibility study and you quickly discover that employee-employer relations are not good. Please discuss how you might use some marketing ideas to get the project off to the right start.

CONTINUING CASE STUDY
Top management has agreed to invest a minimum of $80,000 in a health promotion program in the first year. This is estimated to be approximately one-half the amount of money they will be saving on their health care premiums due to some cost shifting to the employee. A further commitment will be made based on first year performance.

Management has also agreed to allow salaried employees to have flexible hours (flex time) to participate in programs and some programs will include limited time off from normal job responsibilities. Hourly workers can attend lunch hour sessions and ones set up before and after work.

Top management is open to the use of incentives to increase participation in programs in order to decrease absenteeism, and to increase long-term success rate in behavior change workshops. They wish to implement a total ban on work-place smoking as soon as possible. They also are investigating the feasibility of hiring only non-smokers.

The stated reasons top management wants a health promotion program, in descending order of importance are:

1. Decrease health and illness costs.
2. Improve employee-employer relationship.
3. Increase productivity.
4. Provide a safer workplace environment.

They have identified three different categories of program levels to implement; 1) assessment/testing , 2) awareness raising and behavior change, and 3) environmental, cultural and policy supports.

You are part of a task force (planning committee). The task force is composed of a cross-section of employees representing the major interests. Role play one of the following: Top management, Director of Compensation and Benefits, Personnel Manager (the facilitator of the group) Middle Manager (or Supervisor), a non-exempt employee, Manager of employee relations, Assistant to the President.

Questions for Discussion

1. Discuss and write down the mission, three long-term and three short-term goals for this program.

2. As a member of the task force, discuss the concerns (special interests) you have.

3. Top management recognizes the need to distribute a memo concerning the program to all employees. Your committee has been asked for input. What do you feel this memo should say? Please write a sample memo.

4. What health promotion activity(ies) would you implement first?

5. What workplace policies might you consider at the beginning of the program?

6. What incentives or rewards should your task force consider to get your program off the ground? (Remember to address your special interests when discussing the options.)

INTRODUCTION: <u>THE HEALTH RISK APPRAISAL (HRA)</u>

Complete the Health Risk Appraisal Questionnaire which your instructors will give you today. You will begin discussing the computerized results next week and in future weeks. The material below will briefly summarize the important features of the HRA.

Definition of a Health Risk Appraisal

The health risk appraisal is a health promotion activity in which an individual's health related behaviors are evaluated and then compared to other people of his or her age, race, and sex to estimate the risk that individual has of dying in the next 10 years from lifestyle-related causes. The HRA also shows the participant which risks can be improved or eliminated by making positive behavioral changes. Thus, the HRA that you complete can be used as data for both individual wellness decisions and as organizational data for guiding H.P. activities and programs.

Introducing the Center for Disease Control (CDC) Health Risk Appraisal

The Center for Disease Control HRA is one of many popular and widely used HRA instruments. However, we've observed over 200 instruments available, ranging in price from several dollars to several thousand dollars. These forms can be self-scored, scored with a personal computer or batch-computed on micro- and mainframe computers. The personal computer option, like the CDC version, is a nice compromise because it is fairly comprehensive, easy to administer, and the computer software allows a computer printout to be provided for each participant. This printout provides the person with a health age, an achievable age, and a wellness score, as well as other pertinent data.

It also recommends, based on input provided by the participant, specific actions, if any, that he or she can take to alleviate the identified risks.

This appraisal may indicate stress management, smoking cessation, weight reduction, increased exercise, alcohol reduction or abstinence, or other specific behavior changes to reduce the risk of heart disease, cancer, stroke, auto accident or some other cause of death (assess probabilities for disease, injury, or death) The HRA is given confidentially and voluntarily.

What is the Center for Disease Control Health Risk Appraisal (HRA)?
The HRA is a test that is based on your knowledge about your health and lifestyle. It can provide you with some general information about the health risks in your life, using statistics collected from the entire U.S. population. More specifically, it lists the 12 leading causes of death for your race, age, and sex, and estimates the probability of your dying as a result of each of these risk factors within the next ten years.

What are Some of the Limitations of Health Risk Appraisals?
Health Risk Appraisals are still in an early stage of development and there are some limitations. Research on this HRA by the Center for Disease Control is ongoing. One of the most difficult aspects of the process that is used to analyze the HRA data is determining which risk factors contributed to a particular cause of death and to what extent they were influenced by other risk factors. For instance, when someone dies of heart disease, and they were overweight, inactive, and had high blood pressure, how do these risk factors relate to one another as well as to the cause of death? Those and other problems connected with analyzing population statistics (ecological fallacy--generalizing from a population to specific individuals) should produce caution in those using the HRA.

The HRA is not a diagnostic test and should not be used to determine whether or not you have medical problems. We do not recommend that you use this in any way to replace any aspect of your regular medical care. Do not remove yourself from traditional medicine or change any treatment without checking with your MD.

We know that different ethnic groups (i.e. Hispanic) have risk factors that may vary in their importance from the same risk factors in the overall population.

Yet, your test results do not separate these ethnic groups and your printout will reflect only whether your race is White or Black, even though the questionnaire is more specific. Researchers are working on this problem and future versions of the CDC HRA should allow for these differences.

In addition, the HRA may provide data that is too detailed and, hence too costly for use as a baseline for organizational analysis and later evaluation. This may be a problem depending upon your budget, degree of political support, current industry profit picture, size of the organization, and type of ongoing computer support. Once we've decided to move ahead with program development all we really need to know is what interests employees have in various health promotion programs, employee willingness to attend (and when) and something about their health practices, such as how many people have a bad health habit (number that smoke). These insights are very relevant to our later discussion of assessment and planning in module 5.

Given some of the above limitations, what then can this HRA reveal to me about my health? The HRA can show you the statistical probability of your death in the next 10 years of risks factors over which you may have some control and you can change. When viewed in its proper context, the HRA is a valuable personal and organizational tool for assessing risk-producing behaviors, can function as an aid in program evaluation (by analyzing changes over time in the aggregate data collected). It will also provide to you valuable information for choosing effective health behavior interventions and programs, in order to avoid a projected poor quality of life in later years or a premature death. We can see it as one of the many pieces to a wellness puzzle that will provide you with a more complete picture of our present health and life-style.

The Center for Disease Control HRA uses epidemiological data to compare your probability of dying within the next 10 years from the ten or more leading causes of death for your age, race, and sex. Along with the two-page computer printout of your HRA, your instructors may provide you with a Group Summary--a group assessment based on the individual scores of all the members of the class who participated.

Since an HRA deals with health deficits, i.e., your risks of dying, we ask that you also review the results of your TESTWELL wellness inventory. Taking both of these assessments into account when determining your current state of health and well-being, provides you a more balanced, optimistic and personally meaningful result. The lack of positive feedback is a frequent criticism of HRAs by participants who are provided no other measure to assess their health.

How to Read Your First Printout Page--The Top Rectangular Box
The first page of your printout titled "Health Risk Appraisal Program," shows a rectangular box. On the left, the 12 (sometimes more or less) leading causes of death are ranked in order for your age, sex, and race. To the right of each cause of death are four columns. The first column lists the "Average" chance of dying of each of these risk factors in the the next 10 years for everyone in your age, sex, and race group.

The number that appears in that column (and in each of the other columns) are listed as the total number of people who will die per 100,000 persons. A figure of 2654 means that based on the statistics of the general population, for every 100,000 people who are your age, sex, and race, 2654 will die of that risk factor in the next 10 years.

The **second column** shows your "Appraised" age based on the information that you gave us and we fed into the computer. For some people, their "Appraised" age will be lower than their "Average" age, and for others, it will be higher. An "Appraised" score that is higher than your "Average" score usually means that the computer has detected a number of health risk factors in your current lifestyle.

It is important to note that "Average" means just that--the average health status of Americans of your age, sex, and race. What the computer calculates as your "Achievable" age is represented by the third column. If you were to minimize most of the health risks in your life, your score would be close to this. People who have already done so, will show an "Appraised Age" score on their printout that is about the same as their "Achievable Age" score.

Column four, "Differences," simply gives you the difference between your "Appraised Age" score and your "Achievable Age" score. Underneath the top box is a simple line printout concerning your weight. The calculations are based on a medium frame. Since not everyone has a medium frame, the calculation of the percentage that you are overweight (or under weight) are in error, as is the estimate of your desirable weight. Use this only as a general measure and not as an exact indication of what you need to gain or lose.

The Bottom Two Boxes

The box on the left simply lists the positive areas of your lifestyle as indicated by your responses to the questions. The right box shows recommended lifestyle changes. We will discuss these in greater detail below since the second page of the printout deals with these.

How to Read the Second Printout Page

Page two of the printout is titled,"Detail." This page lists the same causes of death that appear on the first page. This time each cause of death has one or more risk factors listed with it. These are listed in the "Condition" column

For example, if heart attack is the number one cause of death, as it is for 45 year old males, the "Condition" column will list blood pressure, diabetes, weight, activity level, smoking, and family history as risk factors related to this cause of death.

To the right of the "Condition" column, the "Appraisal" column will show, based on your answers to the questions, the extent to which each of the "Conditions" contribute to your total risk for that cause of death. For instance, a smoker who quits smoking will definitely reduce his/her risk of a heart attack. However, other risk factors such as blood pressure, weight, and activity level must be considered when assessing the total risk for a heart attack.

The next "Achievable" column shows the same risk factors and indicates what you can achieve by reducing these risks. As with the "Appraised"column preceding it, this column gives a "partial" risk scores and one "total" risk score for each cause of death. The closer your "appraised" numbers are to the "achieved" ones, the less risk you have of dying from that cause of death, based on the computer's calculations.

In the space below, write the important numbers from the first page of your printout.

YOUR HEALTH RISK APPRAISAL SUMMARY

SCORES AND WHAT THEY MEAN

ID. Number:
This is your six-digit code to protect the confidentiality of this appraisal.

ACTUAL AGE:
This is the age you told the computer you were on you last birthday.

APPRAISED AGE:
This is the "health" age the computer calculates you are right now.

ACHIEVABLE AGE:
This is the "health" age the computer calculates you can achieve.

WELLNESS SCORE:

This score is not on your printout, but is easy to determine. It is calculated by taking your "Achievable" score and dividing it by your "Appraised" score. This will give you a percentage score that is usually less than 100%. Ninety percent or above is considered excellent. The following numbers were used to calculate your wellness score:

FORMULA: Achievable Score _____ X
100 = Wellness Score
Appraised Score

WEIGHT:
For your recorded height of   inches, your weight of   pounds is considered   % [] over or [] under weight. (These measurements are calculated on the assumption that you have a medium build and may not be a true reflection of your physical condition.)

Your instructors will provide you handouts detailing the major risk factors and diseases referred to in the CDC Health Risk Appraisal. Review these handouts this week, as well as your HRA results, and get ready to set some personal goals for making positive changes next week.

REFERENCES

Ackoff, R.

1974   *Redesigning the Future: A Systems Approach to Societal Problems.* New York: John Wiley and Sons.

Albert, M. and M. Sullivan

1984   Making Management Philosophy a Cultural Reality, Part I: Get Started. *Personnel*, Jan.-Feb.: 12-21.

Argyris, Chris.

1982   *Reasoning, Learning, and Action: Individual and Organization.* San Francisco, CA: Jossey Bass Publishers.

Ainsworth, Thomas, and O'Donnell, Michael.

1985   *Health Promotion in the Workplace.* New York: John Wiley & Sons.

Albrecht, Karl

1979   *Stress and the Manager.* Englewood Cliffs, N.J.: Prentice-Hall Allen, Robert F.

Allen, Roger J.

1983   *Human Stress: Its Nature and Control.* Minneapolis: Burgess.

American Journal of Health Promotion.

1986,Vol. 1, No. 1

Ardell, Donald W.

1982   *Fourteen Days to a Wellness Lifestyle.* Mill Valley, CA: Whatever Publishing.

Bailey, Covert.

1978   *Fit or Fat?* Boston, MA: Houghton Mifflin Co.

Bellock, N.D. and L. Breslow

1979   Social Networks, Most Resistance, and Mortality: A Nine-Year Follow up Study of Alameda County Residents. *American Journal of Epidemiology.* 109: 186-204.

Bennett, William, and Joel Gurin.

1982 *The Dieter's Dilemma.* New York: Basic Books.

Benson, Herbert.

1975 *The Relaxation Response.* New York: Avon Books.

Bjorntrop, P., L. Sjostrom, and L. Sullivan.

1979 The Role of Physical Exercise in the management of Obesity. In Munroe, J.F. *The Treatment of Obesity.* Lancaster, England: M.T.P. Press.

Brownell, Kelley and Michael R.J. Felix

1988 Competitions to Facilitate Health Promotion: Review and Conceptual Analysis. *American Journal of Health Promotion.* Vol. 2, No. 1: 28-36.

Bureau of National Affairs

1986 *Health Care Costs: Where's the Bottom Line? A BNA Special Report.* Washington D.C.: BNA, Inc. 1986.Burke, Ronald J.

1984 Beliefs and Fears Underlying Type A Behavior: What Makes Sammy Run So Fast and Aggressively? *Journal of Human Stress.* 10: 174-72.

Burks, Nancy and Martin Barclay.

1985 Everyday Problems and Life Change Events: Ongoing versus Acute Sources of Stress. *Journal of Human Stress:* 27-35.

Burnham, John.

1982 American Medicine's Golden Age: What Happened To It? *Science.* 215, March 19: 1474-1479.

1984 The Corporate RX for Medical Costs. *Business Week.* October 15, pp. 138-46.

Cannon, Walter B.

1963 *The Wisdom of the Body.* New York: W.W. Norton:

Caplan, R.D., S. Cobb, and J.R.P. French.

1975 Relationships of Cessation of Smoking with Job Stress, Personality, and Social Support. *Journal of Applied Psychology.* 60: 211-219.

Center for Disease Control.

1985 *Public Health Statistics.*

Cheloha, R.S. and J.L. Farr.

1980   Absenteeism, Job Involvement, and Job Satisfaction in an Organizational Setting. *Journal of Applied Psychology.* 65: 467-473.

Churchman, C.W.

1979   *The Systems Approach and Its Enemies.* New York: Basic Books.

Cleary, P.D., D. Mechanic, and J.R. Greenley.

1982   Sex Differences in Medical Care Utilization: An Empirical Investigation. *Journal of Health and Social Behavior.* 23: 106-119.

Cooper, K.

1982   *The Aerobics Program for Total Well-Being.* New York: M. Evans and Co.

Cousins, Norman.

1984   What You Believe Can Have an Effect on Your Health. *U.S. News & World Report.* Jan. 23: 61-62.

Curtis, John D. and Richard A. Detert.

1981   *How to Relax: A Holistic Approach to Stress management.* Palo Alto, CA: Mayfield.

Daft , Richard

1983   *Organizational Theory and Design.* St. Paul, Minn.: West Publishing Co.

Deal, Terrence E. and Allan A. Kennedy.

1982   *Corporate Cultures: The Rites and Rituals of Corporate Life.* Reading, MA: Addison-Wesley.

DeLongis, Anita, Et.Al.

1982   Relationship of Daily Hassles, Uplifts, and Major Life Events to Health Status. *Health Psychology.* 1: 119-136.

Denniston, O., and I Rosenstock.

1968   Evaluation of Program Effectiveness. *Public Health Reports* 83 (4):323-35.

Dintiman, G.B., S. Stone, J.C. Pennington, and R.G. Davis.

1984   *Discovering Lifetime Fitness.* St. Paul, MN: West Publishing.

Dubos, Rene.

1959   *Mirage of Health: Utopias, Progress, and Biological Change.* New York: Harper and Row.

Dunn, Halbert L.

1961.   *High Level Wellness.* Arlington, VA: R.W. Beatty,

Eckholm, Erick.

1977   *The Picture of Health: Environmental Sources of Disease.* New York: W.W. Norton, Co.

Ellis, Albert and Robert Harper.

1979   *A Guide to Rational Living.* Englewood Cliffs, N.J.: Prentice Hall, .

Ellis, Albert and William Knaus.

1977   *Overcoming Procrastination.* New York: Signet.

Farquar, John W.

1978   *The American Way of Life Need not Be Hazardous to Your Health.* New York: W.W. Norton Co.

Fielding, J.P.

1984   *Corporate Health Management.* Reading, MA: Addison-Wesley.

Fink, A., and J. Kosecoff Eds.

1979   How to Write an Evaluation Report. How to Evaluate Health Programs. Washington D.C.: Capitol Publications.

Finkel, Madelon L.

1985   *Health Care Cost Management: A Basic Guide.* Brookfield, Wisconsin: International Foundation of Employee Benefit Plans.

Freeland, Mark S. and Carol. E Schendler.

1981   National Health Expenditures: Short-Term Outlook and Long-Term Projections. *Health Care Financing Review.* Winter 97-138.

Friedman, Meyer and Diane Ulmer.

1984   *Treating Type A Behavior and Your Heart.* New York: Alfred A. Knopf.

Garfield, Charles.

1986   *Peak Performers: The New Heroes of American Business.* New York: William Morrow.

Gatchel, Robert J. and Andrew Baum.

1983   *An Introduction To Health Psychology.* New York: Random House, Inc.

Girdano, Daniel and George Everly.

1986   *Controlling Stress and Tension: A Holistic Approach.* Englewood Cliffs, N.J.: Prentice Hall.

Ginzberg, Eli.

1983   Cost Containment--Imaginary and Real. *New England Journal of Medicine.* May 19: 1220-23.

Goldsmith, Jeff C.

1980   The Health Care Market: Can Hospitals Survive? *Harvard Business Review.* September/October:.100-12.

Governor's Coalition of Payors to Address Health Care Cost.

1983   Guidelines for Health Insurance Management. Kentucky Employers Handbook on Health Insurance Management Strategies. March: 174.

Green, L. "

1983   Evaluation and Measurement: Some Dilemmas for Health Education. *American Journal of Public Health* 67(2):155-61.

Grossman, J.

1981   Inside the Wellness Movement. *Health.* 13.

Gutknecht, D. and J. Miller.

1986   *The Organizational and Human Resources Sourcebook.* Lanham, MD: University Press of America.

Gutknecht, Douglas B. and David M. Gutknecht

1988   *Designing Health Promotion Systems: Strategies for Individual Wellness and Organizational Health.* Los Angeles, Ca.: HumanResource Press.

Gutknecht, Douglas B.

1985 *Strategic Revitalization: People, Processes and Systems.* Lanham, Maryland: University Press of America.

1988 *Strategic Revitalization: Managing The Challenges of Change.*2nd ed. Lanham Maryland : University Press of America

Hall, Thomas; William Barnes, Mark Stensager, and Lee Carlson.

1984 *Health Care Buyers Guide: A Cost Containment Manual for Purchasers of Health Care Benefits.* Seattle: Health Care Purchasers Association of Puget Sound.

Hay-Huggins Co., Inc.

1985 *Hay-Huggins Benefit Compensation Surveys.* Philadelphia, PA: Hay-Huggins Co., Inc.

Health, United States.

1984 *Mortality Data from the National Center for Health Statistics.* Public Health Service.

Herzlinger, Regina and David Calkins.

1986. How Companies Tackle Health Care Costs:Part III, January/February, *Harvard Business Review*

Herzberg, Mausner B. and B. Syderman.

1985 How Companies Tackle Health Care Cost, Parts II, September/October, *Harvard Business Review*

Kanter, Rosabeth Moss.

1983 *The Change Masters: Innovation for Productivity in the American Corporation.* New York: Simon and Schuster.

Katch, F.I. and W.D. McArdle.

1983 *Nutrition, Weight Control, and Exercise.* (2nd Ed. Philadelphia, PA: Lea and Febiger.

Kerr, Clarke.

1973 Introduction: Industrialism With a Human Face. In Clark Kerr (ed.). *Work in America: The Decade Ahead.* New York: Van Nostrand Reinhold.

Kirscht, J.P.

1983   Preventive Health Behavior: A Review of Research and Issues. *Health Psychology*. 2: 277-301.

Kirscht, J.P. and I.M. Rosenstock.

1979   Patients' Problems in Following Recommendations of Health Experts. In G.C. Stone, et.al. (eds). *Health Psychology: A Handbook*. San Francisco: Jossey-Bass.

Latham, Gary P. and Edwin A. Locke.

1979   Goal Setting--A Motivational Technique That Works. *Organizational Dynamics*. Autumn, 68-74

Lazarus, Richard S.

1984   Puzzles in the Study of Daily Hassles. *Journal of Behavioral Medicine*, 7, 1984: 375-389.

Lewin, Kurt.

1946   Action Research and Minority Problems. *Journal of Social Issues*. 2: 148-163.

McClure, Walter.

1983   Redesigning Benefits Stimulates Cost Consciousness. *Business and Health*. November: 23-26.

McNerney, Walter J.

1980   Control of Health Care Costs in the 1980's. *New England Journal of Medicine*. November 6: 1088-95.

Maslow, A.H.

1970   *Motivation and Personality*. (Rev. ed.). New York: Harper & Row.

1965   *Euspsychian Management: Making Good Management Better*. Homewood, IL: Richard D. Irwin Inc. and The Dorsey Press.

Massachusetts Business Roundtable Report.

1983   *Improving Health Benefits Plan Design*. May.

Moberg, D. Paul.

1984   *Evaluation of Prevention Programs: A Basic Guide for Practitioners*. Wisconsin: Wisconsin Clearinghouse, 1984.

Moberg, S.

1984   *Organizational Health Promotion Evaluation.* New York: Prentice Hall.

Naisbitt, J.

1982   Megatrends. New York: Warner.

Nixon, George.

1973   *People, Evaluation, & Achievement: A Guide to Successful Human Resource Development.* Houston: Gulf Publishing Co.

Odiorne, George S.

1981   *The Change Resistors.* Englewood Cliffs, NJ: Spectrum Books.

1984   *Strategic Management of Human Resources.* San Francisco: Jossey-Bass.

Opatz, Joseph.

1985   *A Primer of Health Promotion: Creating Healthy Organizational Cultures.* Washington D. C.: Oryn Publishing Co.

Ouchi, William.

1981   *Theory Z.* Reading, MA: Addison-Wesley.

Paton, Michael Quinn

1987   *Creative Evaluation.* 2nd. Ed. Beverly Hills, Ca.; Sage Publications.

Pelletier, Kenneth R.

1984   *Healthy People in Unhealthy Places*: Stress and Fitness at Work. New York: Delacorte Press.

Perkins, A.

1981   **The Mind's Best Work**. Boston, MA: Harvard University Press.

Peters, T.H. and R.J. Waterman.

1982   *In Search of Excellence: Lessons From America's Best Run Companies.* New York: Harper & Row.

Rapp, J. and J. Collins

1987   *Maxi-Marketing.* New York: John Wiley and Sons.

Reiser, Stanley.

1978   *Medicine and the Reign of Technology.* Cambridge, England: Cambridge University Press.

Rosenfeld, Isadore.

1987   *Modern Prevention: The New Medicine.* New York: Bantam Books.

Rosenstock, I.M.

1974   The health Belief Model and Preventive Health Behavior. *Health Education Monographs.* 2: 354-386.

Scherer, Greg and Sir Geoffrey Vickers.

1984   *Human Systems Are Different.* New York: Harper & Row.

Scherer, Greg.

1983   *Information packet of Scherer Lumber Company Program.*

Schuster, Frederic E.

1986   *Schuster Reports: The Proven Connection Between People and Profits.* New York: Delta Books.

Scriven, Michael.

1972   The Methodology of Evaluation. In Worthen, B.R. and Sanders, J.R. (eds.) *Educational Evaluation: Theory and Practice.* Belmont, CA: Wadsworth Publishing Co.

Seidel, Victor W. and Ruth Seidel.

1984   *Reforming Medicine: Lessons of the Last Quarter of the Century.* New York: Pantheon.

Seyle, Hans.

1976   *The Stress of Life.* New York: McGraw Hill,

1974.   *Stress Without Distress.* New York: New American Library,

1978   Toward a Theory of Organizational Socialization. In Barry Staw (ed.). *Annual Review of Research in Organizational Behavior.* New York: Jai Press.

Simonson, Maria.

1978   Obesity as a Health Factor. *The Female Patient.* Sept.

Smith, H.W.

1975   *Strategies of Social Research.* Englewood Cliffs, N.J.: Prentice Hall.

Starr, Paul.

1982   *The Social Transformation of American Medicine.* New York: Basic Books, Inc.

Stone, George C., Frances Cohen and Nancy E. Adler.

1979   *Health Psychology.* San Francisco, CA: Jossey Bass, Inc.

Taylor, J.C.

1975   The Human Side of Work: The Socio-Technical Approach to Work Design. *Personnel Review.* Vol. 11, No. 3.

Thigpin, P.

1984   Wellness in the Workplace: Its Role at Levi Strauss and Co. *OD Practitioner.* Dec.

Vickers, Sir Jeffrey.

1984   *Human Systems are Different.* New York: Harper & Row.

von Bertalanffy, L.

1952   *Problems of Life.* New York: John Wiley.

1950   The Theory of Open Systems in Physics and Biology. *Science.* 3: 23-29.

Wallin, L. and I. Wright.

1982   Psychosocial Aspects of the Work Environment. *Journal of Occupational Medicine.* 5: 384-393.

Weber, Max.

1946   *From Max Weber, Essays in Sociology.* Trans. and Ed. by Hans Gerth and C. Wright Mills. New York: Oxford University.

Weick, Karl.

1979   *The Social Psychology of Organizing* (2nd ed.). Reading, MA: Addison-Wesley.

Weil, Andrew.

1983   *Health and Healing: Understanding Conventional and Alternative Medicine.* Boston, MA: Houghton Mifflin, Co.

Windsor, R. A., et. al.

1984   *Evaluation of Health Promotion and Education Programs.* Palo Alto: Mayfield Publishing Co..

Yankelovich, Daniel.

1981   *New Rules: Searching for Fulfillment in a World Turned Upside Down.* New York: Vintage Books.

BIOGRAPHICAL SKETCH OF AUTHORS

Douglas B. Gutknecht is currently an Associate Professor in the Department of Sociology and Director of the Human Resources Development Program at Chapman College in Orange California. He received his P.h. D. from The University of California, Riverside in 1979 and has taught at Pitzer College, The Claremont Colleges, Occidental College, and U.C. Riverside.He will be leaving Chapman College in the Fall of 1989, after teaching there for the past 11 years, to pursue other interests in education, consulting and writing. He and his brother David are the co authors of this text , as well as the co-developers of the innovative, *Wellness Coordinator Certificate Program* that they created in 1985. This program emphasizes the latest research, theory and practice in health and wellness promotion, and fills an existing void in the training of workplace health promotion professionals.

Dr. Gutknecht has published four other books with U.P.A. and has most recently published, **Strategic Revitalization: Managing The Challenges of Change** 2nd. edition in 1988 and and in the Fall, 1989 concurrent with the publication of this text, **The Organization and Human Resources Sourcebook** 2nd. will also be published by U.P.A. In addition to teaching, writing, and consulting, Dr. Gutknecht would like to explore more virorously a career in higher education administration.

David Michael Gutknecht has an M.S. in Counseling Psychology and has consulted widely in the areas of health promotion, group dynamics, improving communication skills and other human resource development topics. He has developed and is marketing with his brother Doug a very unique program called The *C.A.R.E.*(*C*ommunication *A*nd *R*elationship *E*nrichment) *System*. He is currently offering this comprehensive and innovative organizational and people development program to churches and other organizations